The
Mentally Retarded Child
and His Motor Behavior

The Mentally Retarded Child and His Motor Behavior

Practical Diagnosis and Movement Experiences

By

THAIS R. BETER, Ed.D.

Co-Director, Beter-Cragin Private School of Perceptual-Motor Development, Fort Worth, Texas, Formerly Associate Professor of Health, Physical Education and Recreation, Tarrant County Junior College

WESLEY E. CRAGIN, Ph.D.

Co-Director, Beter-Cragin Private School of Perceptual-Motor Development, Formerly Assistant Professor of Health, Physical Education and Recreation, North Texas State University, Denton, Texas

With a Foreword by

Francis Drury, Ph.D.

Chairman, Health and Physical Education Department, Louisiana State University, Baton Rouge, Louisiana

Illustrations by **Nancye Hood**

CHARLES C THOMAS • PUBLISHER
Springfield • Illinois • U.S.A.

Published and Distributed Throughout the World by
CHARLES C THOMAS • PUBLISHER
BANNERSTONE HOUSE
301–327 East Lawrence Avenue, Springfield, Illinois, U.S.A.

This book is protected by copyright. No part of it may be reproduced in any manner without written permission from the publisher.

© *1972, by* CHARLES C THOMAS • PUBLISHER
ISBN 0-398-02230-5
Library of Congress Card Catalog Number: 77-187644

With THOMAS BOOKS *careful attention is given to all details of manufacturing and design. It is the Publisher's desire to present books that are satisfactory as to their physical qualities and artistic possibilities and appropriate for their particular use.* THOMAS BOOKS *will be true to those laws of quality that assure a good name and good will.*

Printed in the United States of America
CC-11

To our parents

FOREWORD

IN RECENT YEARS, there has been a growing awareness on the part of doctors, psychologists, educators and parents that perhaps we have underestimated the potential of mentally retarded children. A specific group of educators, these involved in physical education, has for some time been exploring the concept of the improvement of the mental, social, and physical ability of the mentally retarded in a planned physical education program. Recent research has indicated that these human qualities can be altered through experiences in physical movement. The work of Beter and Cragin is based upon the assumption that many of the mentally retarded children can be helped by participation in a broad area of physical movement. The authors present a complete program, and it should be of great value as a guide for teachers and parents of the mentally retarded youngster.

FRANCIS A. DRURY

PREFACE

THE GREAT AMERICAN ideal of an education for every citizen and a place for each in the family of man is, fortunately, still an influential force in the turbulent 1970's. Governmental legislation has provided the machinery and the funds for public school programs designed to meet the needs of every child, be he gifted, average, or below average.

It is because of our commitment to the American dream of education and our firm belief in the benefits to be derived from movement experiences that we undertook the production of this book. The problems of children with educational disabilities are being attacked at all levels by a diverse group of professionals, governmental agencies and associations of concerned people. It will take a concentrated and cooperative effort of this kind to ultimately provide what is truly *special* education for the thousands of children who are born with, or later develop, neurological impairments, emotional disturbances, perceptual deficits or other mental handicaps.

There is evidence in recent professional literature of a growing realization that present labels or classifications of educational difficulties are not entirely adequate for purposes of planning educational programs. We feel, therefore, that much of the philosophical material in the first two chapters and the diagnostic and program planning information in the rest of the book is applicable to children with all types of learning difficulties. We chose to direct the book toward the group classified as mentally retarded, because we are particularly concerned with their plight and want to present our plea for a more positive attitude by those who plan and guide their learning experiences.

Primarily, the book is designed as a practical guide for anyone who is working with retarded children whether it be in an educational setting, an institutional setting, or a recreational setting. While collecting the data used to set up the norms which appear in the book, we spoke with many special education teachers and visited a number of volunteer recreational programs for the retarded. All of the people involved expressed a desire for information about movement which they could use in their programs. We have also talked to many colleagues in the field of movement education who would like to know more about the mentally retarded child. Information presented in the book is not intended for use only with the higher levels of retardation. We have seen movement experiences used quite effectively with more severely retarded children in a state institution.

Parents of children with learning problems frequently ask if we can prescribe a program that they can follow at home. Although the book is designed for professional people, there are some parts which would be interesting to parents, particularly the underlying philosophy. Many parents are familiar with other programs involving movement that required a very rigorous regimen for the families of retarded children. We want to emphasize, therefore, that neither our philosophy nor the movement experiences we advocate are intended to represent a one-shot panacea for the problems facing a retarded child.

Perhaps the reader who would most appreciate this book is the retarded child himself, and we have attempted, in many instances, to present what we felt was the viewpoint of the child about what he would like done for him.

THAIS R. BETER
WESLEY E. CRAGIN

ACKNOWLEDGMENTS

THE AUTHORS WISH to express their gratitude and appreciation to the many individuals whose concentrated efforts and assistance made this book possible.

Data for the norms which appear in the book were collected by the authors through the testing of children enrolled in a variety of programs throughout the Dallas, Hurst, and Denton, Texas area. This could not have been done without the cooperation of those in charge. We are, therefore, particularly grateful to Miss Verlin Osborne, Executive Director, Dallas Association for Retarded Children; Mrs. Nancy Johnson, former Recreation Director, Dallas Association for Retarded Children; the many recreation assistants at the various centers in the Dallas area; Superintendent of Public Schools in Denton, Texas; Mr. Frank Lindsey and his staff at South Hurst Elementary School, Hurst, Texas.

An affectionate and respectful thanks goes to the many retarded children with whom we enjoyed working and playing, and to the parents of children who aided most graciously.

A very special expression of gratitude goes to Mrs. Michael Walker, our typist, who worked so diligently in the final preparation of the book.

We are also very appreciative of assistance given us by Mr. Naylor Cragin, Mrs. Bobbie Anderson, Mrs. Ann Littlefield and many others in the production of this book.

T.R.B.
W.E.C.

CONTENTS

	Page
Foreword—FRANCIS A. DRURY	vii
Preface	ix
Acknowledgments	xi

1. PHILOSOPHY AND OBJECTIVES OF MOVEMENT ... 3
   Purposeful Concepts ... 3
   Foundation of the Moving, Learning Self ... 4
   Meaningful Means—Practical Objectives ... 7
   Meaning—Centered Developmental
      Objectives of Movement ... 9
   Summary ... 10

2. UNDERSTANDING THE MENTALLY RETARDED CHILD
      AND HIS MOTOR BEHAVIOR ... 11
   Individual Human Behavior ... 12
   Movement Behavior ... 18

3. MEASUREMENT OF GROWTH AND DEVELOPMENT ... 12
   Posture ... 23
   Age, Height, Weight and Anthropometric Measures ... 30

4. MEASUREMENT OF PHYSIOLOGICAL EFFICIENCY ... 41
   Cardiovascular Efficiency ... 41
   Flexibility ... 44
   Muscular Endurance ... 48
   Muscular Strength ... 52

5. MEASUREMENT OF FACTORS IMPORTANT
      IN COMPLEX MOTOR PERFORMANCE ... 60
   Agility ... 60
   Balance ... 64
   Kinesthetic Perception ... 67
   Power ... 74
   Reaction Time and Speed of Movement ... 76

xiv   *The Mentally Retarded Child and His Motor Behavior*

6. MEASUREMENT OF PERCEPTUAL-MOTOR FUNCTIONING   80
   Body-Image   82
   Laterality   85
   Directionality   87
   Temporal Relationships   92
   Sensory Efficiency   98

7. MOVEMENT EXPERIENCES DESIGNED TO DEVELOP FACTORS OF PHYSIOLOGICAL EFFICIENCY AND COMPLEX MOTOR PERFORMANCE   102
   Components of Physiological Efficiency   103
   Relaxation   110
   Posture   112
   Balance   115
   Complex Factors of Motor Efficiency   119
   Circuit and Interval Training   126

8. MOVEMENT EXPERIENCES DESIGNED TO DEVELOP PERCEPTUAL-MOTOR EFFICIENCY   128
   Locomotor Movement Patterns and Basic Motor Skills   130
   Perceptual-Motor Experiences   138

9. SOCIAL PATTERNS OF BEHAVIOR AND LEISURE-TIME ACTIVITIES   149
   Social Patterns of Behavior   149
   Sports, Rhythms and Games for Leisure-Time Enjoyment   152

10. THREE SELECTED CASE STUDIES   161
    Introduction: Where Am I Going?   161
    Case Studies   162
    Summary   177

Bibliography   180
Appendix   187
Glossary   188
Index   191

The

Mentally Retarded Child

and His Motor Behavior

Chapter 1

PHILOSOPHY AND OBJECTIVES OF MOVEMENT

> Blessed are you, when by all these things you assure us that the thing that makes us individuals is not in our peculiar muscles, not in our wounded nervous systems, but in God-given self which no infirmity can confine.
>
> —Author Unknown

PURPOSEFUL CONCEPTS

WHO AM I? What am I? Where am I going? Philosophically, these are three of man's most beautiful, meaningful, yet complex thoughts. Beautiful, meaningful and complex in the respect that all three pertain to man's existence in a universe of "knowing and understanding oneself."

Have you ever asked yourself, What do I feel through, or perhaps, by means of experiences? How do I feel experiences? Are the experiences encountered meaningful? These questions are also relevant to man in his constant quest for truth in order to better understand himself and others.

Thoughts and questions such as these also form the construct for educational endeavors, and the experiences provided by educators become the practicum through which *each* individual develops and utilizes his capacities more constructively toward finding his own truth.

If we now focus our attention on educational endeavors and experiences as they relate to the mentally retarded, we might logically ask a further question. Is the mentally retarded child also in search of truth in this same world of knowing and understanding self? There can be only one answer if we take a positive direction in our thinking. Durant[23] pointed us in the right direction when he suggested that the limit to change or growth is still unknown, and if we could dissolve the preconceived ideas of society, perhaps nothing is really impossible. Continuing in a positive direction, we begin to think and feel that the mentally retarded are more like normal children than they are unlike them. Then we take positive action by rendering, engendering and guiding meaningful experiences for each mentally retarded child so that he may develop his individual potential to its fullest and thus, light his way on the path to self-identification and understanding. Foremost, we need to convey feelings of individual worth: I'm needed, I'm wanted, I'm loved. Effectively conveyed, this becomes the springboard for establishing significant feelings and responses between the retarded child and the individual guiding his experiences.

Positive thinking, then, is the prerequisite to a vital approach in attempting to fulfill individual potentials of the mentally retarded child *in, through*, and *by means* of significant experiences of movement. Hence, "learning to move so we move to learn," as advocated by Metheny[50] is also proposed by the authors as the crux to learning achievement. Moving in purposeful and meaningful ways will further enhance the emotional, social and psychosomatic domains of the mentally retarded. The concept of movement, as introduced in this context, encompasses all human motions (governed by the physical law of force and gravity) in, through and by means of sports, games, dance, exercises, and exploratory movements. Experiences in and through movement are not proposed as ends in themselves, but rather as a most essential means to effective and continuous growth and development.

FOUNDATIONS OF THE MOVING, LEARNING SELF
Who Am I? What Am I?

The foundational structure of the mentally retarded, like any other, is foremost that he is; he is an individual, a human being, a meaningful, useful and total self. He, like us all, possesses the sensitivity of many and varied feelings. This makes him, like the normal (typical) child, an emotional, social, psychosomatic organism who *acts* as an indivisible unit.

What are the implications of this to the learning environment for the mentally retarded child? It means that we must recognize that individuals cannot be treated as a learning mind and a behaving body. There is still a great deal to be learned about the human brain and central nervous system, but it is generally agreed in scientific circles that the idea of separate psychic and somatic entities no longer serves a useful purpose. Studies in psychosomatic medicine are continuing to establish the fact that there is a biological integration which renders mind and body inseparable. In addition, we must understand the learning process and its implications for the mentally retarded. Learning, which has been defined in many ways, is essentially a doing, ongoing process of making sense from what we touch, see, smell, hear and taste. These senses, therefore, along with the kinesthetic sense (awareness of feelings which is provided through the proprioceptors in the muscles, tendons and joints and the labyrinth of the inner ear) are the channels of *input* information which the cognitive processes assimilate. Eventually, the conceptualized data evolve and are represented in overt behavioral patterns. It is through this kinesthetic, or sixth sense, that the authors feel movement experiences can make a very significant contribution toward helping the mentally retarded child find himself. Many authorities in varied fields have also identified this significance and we offer some of their thoughts for your consideration. Steinhaus,[72] a leading physiologist, has said, "Without the sensations that arise from activity in the muscles and joints our 'inner' world of concepts would be flat and completely unreal." He also felt that every "significant experience" is in some way connected with a strong feeling tone and this feeling makes it significant. As Steinhaus[73] sees it, an integrated activity is a significant experience and the only place where the average fellow still gets a totally intergrated experience, one in which the whole individual acts, thinks and feels together, is on the athletic field, playing field or gymnasium. Many people cannot express their feelings as do the poets, musicians or artists, but they can, through feeling experiences in physical activities of movement, find the integration of body, mind and spirit which improves mental health and mental efficiency. This is the peculiarly human role that the muscles take on as a new meaning.

Other expressions of this same idea are presented below.

> Roszak stated that play begins with the child's sensuous manipulation of body . . . and the fun of it all is very fleshy satisfaction. There is a simple and immediate joyousness in the functions and capacities of the body simply for what they are—the body's knowledge and enjoyment of itself is the act of play (Trippet[75]).
>
> In play, by means of play and through play, the probability is great that the true learning potential of the individual is activated (Benoit[10]).
>
> Play weans man from self-centeredness to material objects, to play things, to play fellows, to the group, to the world of people (Oberteuffer[55]).
>
> You cannot teach concepts verbally—you must use a method founded on activity (Piaget[56]).

Moving to learn and learning to move through and by means of purposeful, meaningful experiences is fun; it is play. Have you ever encountered people engaged in joyful and pleasurable movements of one sort or another who were not exhibiting feelings, emotions, desires and drives? Let us cite a few examples and suggest that you momentarily remember some of your own experiences and feelings of movement. Have you *felt* a good swing when contacting a tennis ball with your racket, or golf ball with your golf club? Has the aroma of a beautiful day been actually *felt* and you say, "Gee, it smells good—it feels great"? Perhaps you performed a pivot on the left or right foot and seemingly felt earth's gravitational pull. In attempting a headstand, a handstand or even swinging on a swing or a horizontal bar, you experienced a feeling of your own body in space, in an inverted position or a balanced position. You may have shared the motion of speed or height in running, or riding a wave, swimming, jumping, hopping, leaping; you may have known the feeling of force by making footprints in the sand. Does it not appear, then, that these experiences become a meaningful portion of our repertoire for living, for discovering and exploring relationships, for feeling changes and, therefore, learning through, in and by means of movement? Doesn't it seem plausible that in growing and developing effectively, the mentally retarded child should also build a repertoire of experiences by discovering the body in motion, and that this would assist him more beneficially in answering the questions, Who Am I? What Am I?

It is apparent from what has been presented here that what is involved is not movement for its own sake, but rather, meaningful, purposeful and creative movement experiences. Learning to move so we move to learn is suggested as an essential tool in helping the retarded child to discover and explore *his* feelings, attitudes, desires, needs and emotions in relation to his environment and to make sense of these relationships so that his learning achievement may be enhanced.

Let us remember that no one isolated experience of feeling is demonstrated in overt behavioral patterns. Experiences are cumulative and intertwined with our emotions, feelings and values and they, therefore, determine our actions and reactions. As Axline[5] stated it, ". . . substances of a shadowy world are projected out of our personal thoughts, attitudes, emotions, needs." She further pointed out that "Every individual does have his private world of meaning, conceived out of the integrity and dignity of his personality." Metheny[50] conveyed a similar idea in respect to the importance of movement. She says, ". . . only by moving their bodies can men transform shadow into substance and substance into shadow. Only by moving their bodies can men hope to build the substantial and symbolic temples of their own human understandings."

MEANINGFUL MEANS—PRACTICAL OBJECTIVES

Where Am I Going?

Why are objectives of vital importance to the learning environment? Only through practical goals can we possibly relate the best of scientific knowledge to *each individual pur-*

pose of the mentally retarded. Objectives are the stepping-stones which mark the pathway toward achievement of effective outcomes and toward the observation of overt behavior. These goals become a means, not an end, toward attempting to answer the question, Where am I going? The retarded child will attempt to go to those levels wherein specifically defined goals are progressively and continuously examined and reevaluated in light of the general aim of education: to live productively and serve effectively.

Our reference point, which we must continue to realize, is that of a whole individual socially, emotionally, mentally and physically endowed in a God-given self, with varying degrees of potentialities. In order for the retarded child to possibly achieve and maintain the ultimate in self-fulfillment, diversified channels of guided experiences must be provided, as well as identification of his potentialities through concrete and accurate assessment.

Bearing in mind that all humans do not move alike, some influential factors which may assist in determining immediate objectives are as follow:

1. The structural characteristics of each individual will determine to some extent his capacity for performing various movements.
2. The capability of the individual to engage in movement experiences will be directly related to his development of certain physiological functions.
3. While engaging in movement experiences, the individual will constantly be dealing with physical laws such as gravity, motion and force.
4. Each individual will bring to his movement experiences certain specific characteristics peculiar to his own cultural-familial situation.
5. The individual must utilize his sense modalities for perceiving the world around him.

In essence, we learn to act, interact, and react through sequential, meaningful movements based on individual desires, motivation, physiological conditions and levels of skill.

MEANING-CENTERED DEVELOPMENTAL OBJECTIVES OF MOVEMENT

The objectives are listed below.

1. To present opportunities to move in many ways and for many reasons to develop sensory modalities.
2. To perform exploratory, spontaneous movements for the development of self-expression (problem solving through creativity).
3. To manipulate the body in many positions to determine relationships of space, time, distance, flight, force and gravity.
4. To utilize locomotor movements to enhance everyday movement tasks in living (running, hopping, skipping, leaping and walking).
5. To develop cardiovascular endurance, muscular strength, muscular endurance and flexibility basic to maintenance of optimum health.
6. To engage in movement activities essential to leisure-time enjoyment and social interaction.
7. To motivate and challenge each child through an array of movement experiences for development of the cognitive processes.
8. To provide opportunities through movement to induce relaxation and to reduce tensions for mental health.
9. To present movement experiences for each child to develop various degrees of skill in throwing, catching, batting and kicking.

Based on many observations in the learning environment and on research information, the above movement objectives are proposed by the authors as a means for each mentally retarded child to attain and maintain a fuller, richer and independent life of self-fulfillment. These are tangible objectives of movement for which experiences can be planned and for which outcomes can be easily observed and objectively measured.

The psychological, physiological and sociological implications inferred in the preceding materials are based on what was felt to be sound, scientifically researched findings. These selective facts are by no means all-inclusive or conclusive. They are, however, representative of some of the qualitative information presently available and thereby reflect the authors' viewpoints relative to the mentally retarded child and his search for self in our everchanging society.

SUMMARY

Who am I? I am a purposeful, moving individual of dignity. What am I? I am a feeling individual with emotions, drives, desires, attitudes. Where am I going? I am going where practical, meaningful objectives are attainable through an understanding of the individuals guiding my experiences toward self-fulfillment. The prerequisite to effectively guiding my learning experiences is the means for differentiating and measuring my abilities and capacities.

Start me where I am: to learn to move so I move to learn.

SELECTED READINGS

1. Bell, Virginia Lee: *Sensorimotor Learning—From Research to Teaching.* Pacific Palisades, Goodyear, 1970.
2. Cratty, Bryant J.: *Motor Activity and the Education of Retardates.* Philadelphia, Lea and Febiger, 1969.
3. Espenschade, Anna S., and Eckert, Helen M.: *Motor Development.* Columbus, Merrill, 1967.
4. Lawther, John D.: *The Learning of Physical Skills.* Englewood Cliffs, Prentice-Hall, 1968.
5. Smith, Hope M. (Ed.): *Introduction to Human Movement.* Menlo Park, Addison-Wesley, 1968.

Chapter 2

UNDERSTANDING THE MENTALLY RETARDED CHILD AND HIS MOTOR BEHAVIOR

> If a man does not keep pace with his companions, perhaps it is because he hears a different drummer. Let him step to the music which he hears, however measured or far away.
>
> —THOREAU

IN CHAPTER 1, we laid the philosophical foundations for what we believe can be an effective program of experiences for children with mental handicaps. The authors are both movement educators by training and experience and, therefore, feel quite strongly about the benefits which can be derived from movement experiences. We also feel that this is an area which can be used to help mentally retarded children in a variety of ways. At the same time, we are also cognizant and appreciative of the wealth of theoretical and scientific information being published which contains some support for certain aspects of our philosophy and some opposition.

In the past five to ten years, the interest on the part of professional people in children with a variety of learning disabilities has steadily increased and expanded to embrace a diverse group of special interests. There are psychologists, physicians of many specialties, special educators, physical educators and others all combining their interests and knowledge to discover effective approaches to aiding the retarded child. A logical outcome of such a multidisciplinary effort has been an array of suggested theories for amelioration of learning problems. There also exists at the present time a variety of situations in which people from many fields are working with groups of mentally retarded children. There are public school special education classes, organized community recreation programs, local learning centers, state institutions, private schools, and so forth. The basis upon which the children are selected for these various situations is not uniform, the constituancy of the group in terms of sex, age, background experiences and cultural enrichment is diverse, and the purposes or objectives of the situations are varied. It seems, then, that there is no better time and place than now for us to begin heeding and implementing the principles involved in the concept of individual differences in *learning* and *behaving* which have been developed through years of research. This is our opportunity to serve not as teachers, instructors or directors of learning experiences, but as *human developers*.

INDIVIDUAL HUMAN BEHAVIOR

For those of us in professions which are directly concerned with guiding or measuring human behavior, we have been forced more times than not to deal with group behavior rather than individual behavior. In order to gain knowledge about some aspect of behavior, we take a group of people and measure or observe them on a particular task and, based on a relatively large number of results, a criterion is established which represents the norm as reflected by the way the largest percentage of the group performed. When subsequent individuals are measured or observed on this same task, we compare their performance to the norm and conclude that they are subaverage, average or above average.

The authors feel that in order to effectively utilize the concepts of individual differences, particularly with mentally retarded children, it is necessary to go beyond the bounds of our usual procedures. Because of the extremely complex nature of human behavior, any individual's performance on any task is affected by such a multiplicity of factors that we are still far from reaching a complete understanding of what that performance truly reflects. It is our feeling that the interaction of these factors does not obscure true ability in the average child as much as it might confuse interpretation of performance by the atypical child. As explained by Ames,[3] "In many instances, and with regard to many behaviors, the supposedly abnormal is not completely different from the supposedly normal, but may often be merely a behavior which is immature for the individual in question." Having to analyze and interpret the performance of one individual by comparing it to what is known about normal behavior and at the same time recognize and credit the aspects which are unique to this individual is one of the most difficult tasks with which teachers have always had to deal. The human developer will find it even more difficult, but it is a task which must be dealt with in working with the mentally retarded child.

As a start in the discussion of what we feel is the best approach to understanding the motor behavior of mentally retarded children, we would like to first briefly review the general setting as it exists at the present time concerning the appraisal and understanding of the behavior of these children.

Many attempts have been made to adequately define mental retardation and to devise systems for classifying children with diagnosed deficiencies. At the present time, both the definitions and classifications give us a base from which to operate, but most authorities agree that neither is entirely adequate. The difficulty involved was summed up by Hutt and Gibby[35] when they said, "Mentally retarded children are individuals in their own right, and we can talk about 'the' mentally retarded child only as an abstraction . . . ." We are not going to attempt to review the various approaches to classifications or categories, but some basis for our discussion is necessary. We think that some of the information from a manual prepared by the American Association for Mental Deficiency[74] might be the most helpful in setting the framework for an understanding of the children for whom you will be developing movement behavior. The theoretical definition of mental retardation is given in the manual as follows:

> Mental retardation refers to subaverage general intellectual

functioning which originates during the developmental period and is associated with impairment in adaptive behavior.

As further elaboration of the definition, the manual goes on to explain some of the ways in which impaired adaptive behavior might be determined.

1. During the preschool years, particularly, manifestations of impaired adaptive behavior may be evident in delayed acquisition of developmental skills such as sitting, crawling, walking, talking, habit training and interaction with age peers.

2. During the school years, impaired adaptive behavior would be reflected in learning difficulties manifested in an inability to acquire knowledge as a function of experience.

3. Impaired adaptive behavior can also be reflected in social adjustment at all levels. During the preschool and school years the level and manner in which a child relates to parents, other adults, and age peers is an indication of his social adjustment. In the adult it would be reflected by the ability to function independently in the community, to be gainfully employed and to accept responsibilities.

This represents a very good framework for beginning to understand the mentally retarded child, but a real understanding requires that we examine these basic guidelines a little further. The above procedure provides a sound basis for making a diagnosis that a given individual is mentally retarded, but except for the element of degree, the items mentioned are not distinctive to retarded children. The normal school population may be represented by intelligence quotients which fall above one standard deviation below the mean, but this does not assure that all of these children are functioning at their intellectual potential. Also, learning difficulties and poor social adjustment are evident in all groups of students at all educational levels. The point we want to emphasize here is that what we are most concerned with is not any one distinct group of children, but with identifying specific hang-ups in the learning process with each child. If a child has a visual-perception problem, it does not really matter whether his IQ falls at the mean level, three standard deviations below or three standard deviations above the mean. What is important is knowing that the visual-perception problem exists and attacking it with appropriate methods.

Much of the literature geared for special education focuses a major emphasis upon how to deal with exceptional children in terms of their disabilities and limitations. There are pages and pages of detailed descriptions concerning what you *cannot* expect these children to do and detailed descriptions concerning characteristics attributed to these children which represent deterrents to effective learning. As a result of what might be termed a clinical approach to trying to describe the causes of learning disabilities, we have unconsciously come to adopt a somewhat clinical approach to diagnosing abilities and planning learning experiences for exceptional children. If a child comes to someone working in the area of special education, and if he is suspected of being mentally retarded or brain-injured, or if his physical appearance identifies him as a mongoloid, that worker will quite likely immediately begin to think in terms of the child's handicap and the limitations of performance which have been established as associated with the handicap. Inadvertently, then, a negative kind of atmosphere is built around both the child and the educator. Too often this kind of atmosphere will result in our failure to obtain all of the relevant information necessary to a complete understanding of the child, and probably failure also to plan the most appropriate learning experiences for him. The fact that the term "exceptional children" is used, of course, means that children who fall in this category will usually exhibit one or more characteristics which deviate from what we have come to think of as standard behavior. Within this predetermined classification, however, we feel that it is important to remain positive and unbiased in any expectations concerning the performance of these children.

It seems, then, that the perceptual view of human behavior provides the best approach to understanding the mentally retarded child. With this view, we look at human beings not only through our own eyes, but also in terms of the behaving person himself and we recognize that any individual behaves at any particular time in relation to the way things seem to him at that moment. There are many aspects of perceptual functioning as it relates to behavior, and a number of definitions have been offered to explain the concept. The emphasis in all of these definitions is the idea that perception is a process involving the recognition, organization and interpretation of stimuli from an individual's immediate environment. These stimuli enter through the sensory modalities and are conveyed to the central nervous system; the result is some overt response. The perceptual act is very complex and its many branches intertwine with a variety of other factors related to total behavior. There is still much that is not known about the perceptual act, about human behavior, or about the relationship between the two.

There is considerable authoritative support for using perception as the basis for understanding human behavior, for diagnosing deviant behavior and for planning experiences to ameliorate learning problems. The broad school of perception advocates, however, splinters into separate departments when it comes to *how* perception is related to behavior and learning.

In psychological history, the development of perceptual theories would start with Berkeley's theory[11] of space perception which was indicative of the view, prevalent at that time, that everything we know comes to us through our senses. Continuing this same basic viewpoint, the associationists added to it by suggesting the combination of different sensory information to form ideas. The major change from the sensory experience point of view occurred with the emergence of the Gestalt school. Gestalt theorists viewed perception as being "sensory fields" rather than small sensory parts. The most recent attempts to explain behavior or intellectual development come from the developmental psychologists. As a contemporary spokesman, Piaget[56] has identified certain developmental stages which he feels are influenced by both sensory and motor experiences as well as by genetic factors.

The literature dealing with sensory and perceptual aspects of behavior is so extensive and complex that it almost defies condensation or summarization. Actually, theoretical direction toward understanding perceptual behavior is still essentially unresolved. Some very important questions pertaining to the behavior of retarded children remain to be answered, such questions as How much of retarded behavior at chronological ages eight, nine and ten is capable of being ameliorated? Can sensory experience through one modality enhance learning which has been affected by sensory deprivation in another modality?

In addition to the lack of some specific information, some of the divergence in current theories undoubtedly stems from disciplinary bias and some from the fact that practical experiences just do not follow the theoretical blueprint. This latter point is one which we feel should be examined a little more closely. The gap between theory and practice is an old thorn in the side of education and it seems to be rearing its ugly prong in the case of special education. A very lively topic of discussion in professional circles concerned with retarded children centers around the question of how beneficial programs of motor development are in enhancing retarded intellectual functioning. There is the inevitable discussion of the continually low correlations obtained between mental and motor abilities. The final solution of this controversy, of course, is deeply embedded in the mystery of perception, central nervous system function and human behavior. For the moment, however, it seems that the discussion is really just academic. Certainly the suggestion that a fourteen-year-old mentally retarded child spend two hours a day crawling around on the floor so that he can improve his reading ability lacks scientific credence. If we are going to accept the idea that it is the total child to whom we are directing our attention, however, then does it really matter what approach was used if the result is satisfactory in terms of favorably changed behavior in the child? There is much scientifically based information available for us to use in directing our efforts on behalf of mentally retarded children, and we should certainly use as much of it as we can. It also seems that until we find more complete answers, it would be well to rely on practical results as some measure of success.

MOVEMENT BEHAVIOR

In the preceding material, we have tried to present a very abbreviated review of the current situation as it relates to understanding the mentally handicapped child. The question of where movement experiences fit into a diagnostic and remedial program for children with learning or behavior problems is still subject to answers representing controversial viewpoints. Because of our experience working in the area of movement education, the authors feel that appropriate movement experiences are a very vital part of the perceptual development of any child. We further feel that it is not really necessary to choose one particular theory of perceptual-motor development, but that it is probably more beneficial to be cognizant of both the similarities and differences evident in each of the approaches suggested. Anyone who has had experience working with groups of children of any description knows that one method of presenting material or of eliciting responses is never adequate for all individuals within the group. Certainly this same principle is applicable in dealing with retarded children. We must keep in mind that our task is to take any individual child and, within the framework of his equipment, help him to become a perceiving, behaving person.

We tried to point out previously that within any group of ten mentally retarded children, we could find ten variations in terms of why these children have been considered to be different in behavioral patterns. One may have neurological dysfunctioning that affects auditory perception, another may have faulty visual perception, a third impaired motor functioning and another may simply lack past experiences in play activities. As a group category, these are children who exhibit some degree of impairment in adaptive behavior which would result from a variety of syndrome-type patterns in their developmental periods.

The approach we are suggesting is that until additional scientific information becomes available which clearly points the way toward *the* best solution, our most intelligent approach is to assess each child in a manner which will tell us what he can do and what he cannot do. We then take advantage of what he can do, and plan experiences to enrich those areas where he is presently deficient. In order to do this, we feel that there are several broad areas of movement behavior which lend themselves to both diagnosis and prescriptive programs, and these will be developed in more detail in later chapters.

Perception

Until evidence is presented which unequivocally refutes the relationship of movement, perception and intelligence, we feel that it should be considered an important area of consideration in programs for the mentally retarded. Denhoff[20] has identified the motor bases for perceptual development as follow:

1. Posture.
2. Directionality.
3. Laterality.
4. Awareness of position of the body in space.

These are essentially the same factors recognized by Kephart[39] and other advocates of perceptual-motor development. As a first step in understanding the movement behavior of a child, then, it would be necessary to establish the degree of his progress in the areas representing the framework for more complex motor behavior.

Motor Planning

If a child appears to have reached adequate development in the areas representing the motor bases of perception, the next step in evaluation would involve his proficiency in what

Ayres[6] has described as motor planning. This level of motor behavior involves goal-directed movement which results in feedback that serves to improve the ability to motor plan. Ayres recognizes four sensory modalities that are important to skilled motor planning. These are touch, proprioception, vestibular function and vision. In addition to evaluating performance in goal-directed movements, it would also be beneficial to examine the child's use of each of these senses independently.

Basic Movement Patterns and Coordination

There may be some children who will not evidence any observable difficulty on tasks included in the previous categories and yet will be unable to adequately perform some of the basic movement patterns. We suggest, then, that although there is some overlapping, it would still be helpful to assess abilities involved in locomotive movement patterns of hopping, skipping, jumping, and in basic gross motor skills of hitting, kicking, throwing and catching.

Physiological Functioning

Muscular strength and muscular endurance, particularly of the arms, legs and abdomen, cardiovascular efficiency and flexibility are factors of physiological functioning that are important to everyone in dealing with the demands upon the body. For some mentally handicapped children, this is a very vital area to evaluate. It depends, of course, upon the nature of the handicap as well as other factors, but many of these children lead relatively restricted lives in terms of opportunities for physical activity and an evaluation of their status in this area is very important.

Motor Performance

There are some factors of motor ability which physical educators consider to be important in the performance of the complex movements involved in sports activities. There will be children, paricularly in special education classes in the public schools who are capable of learning the skills necessary for engaging in many sports. It is therefore necessary to be able to evaluate their potential for success in these experiences, and this would involve assessing abilities such as reaction time, speed of movement, agility, power, kinesthetic perception and rhythm.

Chapter 3

MEASUREMENT OF GROWTH AND DEVELOPMENT

The body represents the individualization
of my engagement in the world.
—SARTRE

IN THE BEGINNING, there is that factor which dictates our movement—the human structure—which in the last 210,000 years has evidenced little, if any, change. A second factor which affects our movement is the everpresent pull of earth's gravity and the physical laws which govern our existence.

Growth is usually assigned to the measurable physical and biological changes in the individual's development, while *maturation* is subject to more divergent opinions among authorities. Although no universally accepted definition exists presently, the term "maturation" is most frequently used to describe those changes which develop in an orderly fashion, without direct influence of known external stimuli, but which are almost certainly, in part at least, a product of the interaction of the organism and its environment. The processes of growth and maturation proceed apace toward the development of behavior necessary for continued successful functioning of the organism.[26]

These aspects are brought to focus by the authors because, as the child moves at his own rate and in his own way through the process of human development, each stimulus and response tends to expand to various degrees his own capacities.[26] Furthermore, the important interrelationships of his function to his structure dictates vital needs for all types of movement activities (sensory motor).

Is it not visually observable that some boys as well as girls of the same chronological age appear to be the same height and perhaps the same weight? Seemingly, we also notice differences in height and weight (size and shape) in individuals of the same age. Consequently, performances of people are influenced by height, weight, and body structure. Some people differ in body weight, but they are of the same height. Others, though weighing the same, have relatively unequal proportions of muscle, fat and bone. As Ames[3] pointed out, "It is important for anyone who deals with the human organism in any capacity to keep in mind that behavior has shape; it is a function of structure, and that we behave as we do largely because of the way we are built."

POSTURE

Posture means the relative *position* of the body, taking into consideration the correlation of the skeletal, muscular and nervous systems. Briefly stated, posture literally is a position. Man in his upright posture will govern the ways in which he experiences the world. To maintain that which is considered an *erect* posture requires that we continually fight the force of gravity and in so doing, perceive space from a necessitated postural equilibrium.

It should be noted that posture is largely a matter of *habit*. If good, it contributes to the appearance and efficiency of the body; it spoils the appearance and makes the body inefficient, if bad. Good or bad, if a given posture is assumed often enough, a neuromuscular response is established which becomes typical of a person.[49] Another factor to remember relative to posture is that, at rest or in motion, a person often reveals the image which he has of himself and expresses the attitude with which he faces certain situations of living.[51]

Posture is also an individual thing. Metheny[49] stated the following regarding the individuality of posture: "There is no single best posture for all individuals. Each person must take the body he has and make the best of it. For each person the best posture is that in which the body segments are balanced in the position of least strain and maximum support. This is an individual matter." Goldwaite and others[30] concurred when they concluded that there is not and cannot be one posture which is normal for all individuals and to which all individuals should conform.

Body posture also affects and depicts physiological functions. For instance, energy requirements of different postures vary considerably. About 20 percent more energy is required for a rigid military posture than the easy standing position, and an extremely relaxed standing position requires 10 percent less energy than an easy standing position. It is known that the blood pressure rises when a person assumes an erect, rigid posture because of the muscular effort involved. Consequently, from the physiological point of view, the efficiency of the rigid, erect posture is not normal due to the reduction in the metabolic and circulatory systems. Another factor which produces physiological change, considered to be pathological, is extreme curvature and malalignment. It can be noted, however, that minor deviations do not seem to greatly affect the health and efficient functioning of the internal organs.[17]

Some examples of differences of posture, illustrating the above factors are the pompous stride of the weighty man which signifies that perhaps he carries a heavy burden and sustains it well; the identification of the military man which expresses discipline, authority and pride in his upright position; and the inflexible posture of a dictator which may suggest that he is seeking to impress his inflexible will upon the consciousness of his people.[51]

The important points of emphasis from the foregoing can be summarized as follow:

1. The concept of normal posture is a condition in which the organs and systems of the body function efficiently.

2. Posture is an *individual* matter.

3. Individuals' attitudes and habits are reflected in their postural positions.

Measurement of Growth and Development

4. Different postural positions require varying amounts of energy.

5. Man governs the ways in which he experiences the world in his upright position.

Evaluation (Posture Tests)

The standing posture represents a practical approach in the assessment of body alignment. Although standing is only one of many postures assumed daily, this evaluative procedure can serve as a point of departure for assessing many points rather quickly and accurately.

Gravity Test (Plumb Line Test [63])

The gravity test is described below:

1. The plumb line: An ordinary string is suspended freely overhead with some small weight attached to the bottom. The weight does not touch the floor and the suspended string will serve as a visual guide for the line of gravity.

2. Side view: With the individual's side next to the plumb line, but not touching, have him assume his own *comfortable, normal standing* posture so that the plumb line dissects his body into two approximately equal halves—front and back. *Avoid* "standing straight"—this is not an evaluation of what *should* be, but of what *is*.

3. Back view: The person stands with his back to the plumb line and is centered so that the line dissects his body into two symmetrical halves—right and left. The plumb line will appear to follow the line of his spinal column and drop directly between his legs and feet. Again, this position is not what *should* be, but what is *natural*.

When you have placed the student in the positions described above, use the following checklist to evaluate the posture from both the side and back views.

CHECKLIST FOR ASSESSMENT OF STANDING BODY ALIGNMENT *

Side View	Normal Alignment	Deviations
1. Body weight	Centered over the feet _____	Forward over the balls of the feet _____
		Backward over the heels _____
2. The body	Extended comfortably as a whole _____	Slumped _____
3. Head	Balanced over shoulders _____ (from the lobe of the ear to the tip of the shoulder, a vertical line should be visible)	Tilted forward _____
		Tilted backward _____
4. Shoulders	Balanced over hips _____ (a vertical line should be visible from the tip of the shoulder to the center of the hip joint)	Shifted forward _____
		Shifted backward _____
5. Chest	High _____ (should not appear overly expanded)	Depressed _____
6. Upper back	Slightly rounded _____ (the appearance of the upper back in its normal "habitual" position)	Markedly rounded _____
		Flat _____
7. Shoulder blades	Flat _____ (check again from back view)	Protruding (wings) _____
8. Lower back	Normal curve _____ (curve of the spine-lumbar region)	Flat _____
		Hollow _____
9. Abdomen	Slightly rounded _____ (characteristic of women) Flat _____	Protruding _____
10. Knees	Easy _____ (slightly flexed)	Hyperextended _____ (locked)
		Bent too much _____

Measurement of Growth and Development

CHECKLIST Continued

Back View	Normal Alignment	Deviations
1. Head	Centered_____(directly centered over shoulders)	Tilted right_____
		Tilted left_____
2. Shoulders	Even or level_____	Right low_____
		Left low_____
3. Hips	Even or level_____ (check the spaces between the arms and the body at the level of the hips)	Right low_____
		Left low_____

* Courtesy of Shrader, Ray Anne: Action models for functional fitness. In Smith, Hope M. (Ed.): *Introduction to Human Movement.* Menlo Park, Addison-Wesley, 1968.

Results of an alignment check will be more valuable and will represent a more accurate evaluation if these assessments are repeated more than once. Although your initial evaluation may be essentially accurate, practice will make it more perfect.

Assessment of Muscle Shortening [63]

Another area of utmost importance in posture assessment involves the muscle groups which are primarily responsible for body alignment maintenance. Shrader[63] stated that shortening in a given muscle group may not be a cause of specific postural deviations, but tight muscles do resist postural correction.

Test 1 (calf of the leg): Sit on the floor with the legs closed and extended. The weight of the upper body is rested on the hands while leaning back slightly. Keep the knees extended and attempt to dorsiflex (pull toward the body) the ankles to right angles.

Test 2 (back of the thigh): Lie on the back, stretch the arms out comfortably at shoulder-level with the palms facing upward on the floor. Bend the elbows and rotate at the shoulder joint until the forearms are at right angles to the upper arms with the backs of the hands and forearms still resting on the floor. Lift *only* one leg into the air, keeping the knees of both legs straight. Keep flexing at the hip until the lifted leg is at a 90° angle with the body. Repeat the lifting action with the other leg.

Test 3 (hip flexors): Lie on the back and pull with the arms the thigh of one leg to the chest. Keep the other leg extended on the floor with the knee *extended*. Repeat the movement with the other leg.

Test 4 (lower back): Take a sitting position with the knees extended. Reach for the toes and attempt to touch them with the fingertips.

Test 5 (chest): Lie on the back and clasp the hands behind the head. Flex the knees slightly. While in this position, the elbows should be resting on the floor without any strain.

CHECKLIST FOR USE WITH TESTS 1 THROUGH 5
OF MUSCLE SHORTENINGS *

Good—can do the test with ease.
Fair—Feels some strain.
Poor—feels great strain or cannot do it.

Test	Encircle the Appropriate Letter		
1. Calf of leg—gastrocnemius and soleus	G	F	P
2. Back of thigh—hamstring muscles	G	F	P
3. Hip flexors	G	F	P
4. Lower back—lumbar extensors	G	F	P
5. Chest—pectoral muscles	G	F	P

* Courtesy of Shrader, Ray Anne: Action models for functional fitness. In Smith, Hope M. (Ed.): *Introduction to Human Movement*. Menlo Park, Addison-Wesley, 1968.

Considerations for Assessment

Some considerations for assessment are as follow:

1. Postural deviations may be classed as *functional* or *structural*. In functional conditions, only the muscles and the alignment are affected and correction is possible by controlling the positions of the body through exercise and conscious, habitual positions. One must *learn* through movement experiences to develop an awareness or "feel" for what is balanced alignment and to incorporate this series of sensations into

postural habits. Suggested exercises for posture and muscle shortening improvement are to be found in a later chapter. *Structural* conditions exist when the bony structure has been changed or affected. Correction for structural conditions is the province of the physician, who may resort to surgery or casting, or both, in an effort to secure desired improvement.

2. Due to the mentally retarded child's lack of kinesthetic awareness (feel of body position), it is suggested that some time be devoted to spot checks of the various areas that are being assessed. Perhaps a movement of the specific part of the body (in or out, to or away from the body) with assistance may prove more beneficial for accurate evaluation in certain areas.

These tests have been selected because of their practicality and ease of administration. Other tests recommended by the authors are as follow: Iowa Posture Test and Woodruff Body Alignment Posture Test. There are, of course, many other tests available, but they require experienced evaluators and prove to be more expensive than the above noted. Those who desire further information are referred to the suggested sources at the end of this chapter.

A Brief Review of Selected Related Research

Hutchins,[34] in a recent study, found evidence of a relationship between selected strength and flexibility variables and concluded that the balance of strength between trunk-flexor and trunk-extensor muscles and other muscle groups was an important factor in anteroposterior alignment. Evidence was further reported in her study to support the current posture-training methods involving specific strength and flexibility exercises.

Other investigators have attempted to study the relationship between posture and various physiological and emotional characteristics. Alden and Top[1] investigated the relationship of posture to the factors of weight, vital capacity and intelligence. No relationship was found between posture and the variables investigated. A significant relationship between poor posture and certain physical and emotional factors, including self-consciousness, fidgeting, restlessness, timidity, fatigue, underweight, disease, heart defects, hearing problems and asthma was reported by Moriarity and Irwin.[52] In an earlier study, Spindler[70] concluded that there was a need for corrective and remedial work.

AGE, HEIGHT, WEIGHT AND ANTHROPOMETRIC MEASURES

The public education system in the United States has customarily depended upon chronological age as a single classification factor for placement of students. With the advent of organized special education classes in the public school, attention has been given to the mental age of the students, but placement is still to some extent determined by chronological age.

There have been isolated indications from various sources in recent years that all educators are recognizing that exact chronological age is not necessarily the best indication of how a child will perform mentally, socially, or emotionally. Physical educators for many years have realized that physical performance is dependent upon a combination of factors. Anthropometric measurement provided the early understanding of physical performance and research in this area, and has shown that complete evaluation of physical maturity should be based on an examination of age, height, weight, body size and shape.

To do a complete and reliable job of measuring in these areas unfortunately requires special knowledge and skill, and some of the measurements require a great deal of time to administer. Because this is such a fundamental and vital area of physical measurement and because it contributes toward the complete understanding of the total child and his behavior, the authors felt that it should be discussed. We have included some references to the most valid ways of measuring in these areas for those who may have the experience necessary to do it. We have also included some simpler ways of making an assessment, which are presented because they can serve as a broad screening procedure to help call attention to possible problems.

Physiological Age

As previously mentioned, educators have customarily used chronological and mental ages as the basis for planning educational experiences for children. Another important indicator of the maturity of growing children is the physiological age. Research has shown that there can be a significant difference between the chronological age and the physiological maturity of children. Clarke and Wickens[15] found that within a group of forty 10-year-old boys, the physiological ages ranged from eight years and less to twelve years and more. The most valid method for determining the physiological maturity of a child is by determining his skeletal age. The procedure for determining skeletal age involves the use of hand and wrist x-rays and would, therefore, be impractical for most school situations. Many diagnostic centers do include this measurement in their overall evaluation of children and the information might possibly be available to the teacher or others working in programs with mentally retarded children. There are some other less complicated methods of obtaining a general indication of the maturational level of children and they can serve a useful purpose as further pieces in the total picture of the child being evaluated.

Dental Age

The maturational level of prepubescent boys and girls is related to the eruption of the permanent teeth. The dental age is obtained by determining the number of permanent teeth which have appeared and comparing it to norms for that age. For example, in the chart shown in Table I, the appearance of nine permanent teeth is normal for boys at age eight. If you had a boy who had only nine permanent teeth and who was chronologically ten years old, this could be an indication of retarded physical development.

TABLE I

NORMS FOR APPEARANCE OF PERMANENT TEETH
IN BOYS AND GIRLS

Number of Permanent Teeth Appearing		Dental Age
Boys	Girls	
2–3	2–3	6
6	7	7
9	10	8
12	13	9
15	17	10
19	21	11
23	25	12
26	27	13

Courtesy of Clarke, H. Harrison: *Application of Measurement to Health and Physical Education,* 4th ed. Englewood Cliffs, Prentice-Hall, 1967.

Pubescent Development

Physical maturity of boys and girls who have entered adolescence can be obtained by assessing certain aspects of their pubescent development. Research has shown that there is a high correlation between physical growth and appearance of menarche in girls. Generally speaking, the earlier the start of menstruation, the more rapid the physical growth. Physical maturity of adolescent boys can be determined by assessing the secondary sex characteristics. The first sign of impending puberty is usually an acceleration in the growth of the testes and scrotum, with slight growth in pubic hair beginning at the same time.

Height, Weight and Body Size

For many years, people in all walks of life faithfully checked the popular age-height-weight charts and smiled or groaned accordingly when they determined that they were over- or underweight. Investigations in this area have since shown that height and weight alone do not give the whole picture. Simple observation of a group of individuals will reveal a wide variety of shapes and sizes. How the weight or height of an individual is distributed is of much greater interest than the single measure of either. Changes in both height and weight, of course, are important indices during the growing years and both measures can be important data in adult assessment of physical status. Some of the important points in obtaining these two measurements are therefore reviewed.

Weight

The platform scale is considered to be the most accurate measure of weight and should be used whenever possible. Bathroom scales, although better than no measurement, have been found to fluctuate and to be less accurate than the more stable, platform-type scale. There are many things which can affect the body weight, and sources concerning the procedure for obtaining weight vary in the instructions given. The most important principle to remember is that of consistency of method. The amount of clothing worn, whether the shoes are left on or removed, the time of day, and so forth should be the same each time the child is weighed.

Height

The sliding rod with horizontal arm at the top, which is found on most platform scales, is the least accurate method for measuring height. A stadiometer is recommended as the best way to get accurate height measures, but this equipment will probably be unavailable to many of the readers. A permanent measuring station can be made, however, which can serve just as well. A scale can be marked off on the wall so that height measurements can be recorded to the nearest one-fourth inch. If the scale is put on the wall, the baseboard and any other projections must be removed so that the student can stand with heels, buttocks and head flat against the wall. Also, an object should be used to press firmly down on the student's head and to form a right angle to the wall for reading the scale.

Anthropometric Measures

The anthropometric measures which are usually taken, along with height and weight, are chest depth, hip width, arm and leg girth and shoulder width. There are appropriate charts and formulae which have been devised for use with these measurements in making a decision concerning the body structure. The most accurate method of obtaining these measurements is with calipers and special measuring tapes. Since this equipment will not be readily available, the procedure will not be discussed here. Special references are given at the end of the chapter, however, for those who would like to include these measures in their program.

The major concern of those who will be working with retarded children is probably that of detecting those individuals who are approaching or have attained a problem degree of obesity. Jean Mayer[47] has pointed out the important distinction between overweight and obesity. He defines obesity as "excessive accumulation of body fat," and overweight as "weight in excess of normal range." This, of course, emphasizes the point previously made. A person might be overweight when compared to others of the same age and height, but this may not be a deviant condition when this individual's overall body size and proportions are considered.

Instead of making a determination on the basis of overweight as it was previously defined, some of the readers may prefer to use a simple test for obesity. Much of the recent literature, actually, is suggesting that the amount of excess fat is the factor with which we should be concerned. Instead of trying to make comparisons on the basis of age, height, weight and body build, one simply measures the excess fat of each individual and uses this to make a decision as to whether that person has a problem. Mayer[47] has suggested several methods for determining excess fat, and although they cannot be considered as being as scientific as methods involving special equipment, they can at least point out a potential problem. Two of these methods are given below.

THE PINCH TEST. It has been estimated that about half of the body fat is located directly under the skin in individuals under the age of fifty. At certain areas of the body, a fold of skin and subcutaneous fat can be lifted between the thumb and forefinger, thus separating it from the underlying soft tissue and bone. The areas which are most frequently used are the back of the upper arm, the side of the lower chest, just below the shoulder blade on the back, and the abdomen. A fold in any of these areas which is decidedly greater than one inch would indicate excessive body fatness; one which is considerably less than one-half inch would indicate abnormal thinness.

THE RULER TEST. An examination of the slope of the abdomen can also be an indication of excessive fat. When a person lies on his back, the surface of the abdomen will be flat or slightly concave if he is not too fat. By placing a ruler on the abdomen along the midline of the body, one can test the degree of excess fat. If the fat is normal, the ruler should touch both the ribs and the pelvic area.

Determination of Body Type

The relationship between body build and human behavior has been a subject of interest since the days of Hippocrates. This interest in body types has ranged from the thorough, complex study done by Sheldon[62] to the literary references of Shakespeare to the "lean and hungry look" of Cassius as an indication that "he thinks too much."

Constitutional psychology recognizes the role that morphology and physiology play in overall human behavior, and the authors felt that some attention should be given to this aspect of physical measurement. Although the classification of individuals into specific body types is a technique which requires some skill and experience, there are shorter methods for at least identifying the basic body build. The three most commonly used body types are as follow:

Endomorphy

This is the classification used to describe the extreme body type which is characterized by a predominance of soft roundness of various parts of the body, particularly around the trunk area. Other identifying characteristics of the endomorph would be a round head, short neck, narrow shoulders, fatty breasts, short arms, wide hips, heavy buttocks and short, heavy legs.

Mesomorphy

This is used to describe the well-developed, muscular individual who is usually considered the typical athletic type. The mesomorphic person has prominent facial bones, a long but muscular neck, wide shoulders, muscular arms and forearms, broad chest, heavily muscled abdomen, low waist and narrow hips, muscular buttocks and powerful legs.

Ectomorphy

This represents the extremely fragile and linear body type. This type is characterized by small bones, large forehead, a long skinny neck, narrow chest, round shoulders with winged scapulae, long slender arms, flat abdomen, small buttocks and long, thin legs.

The above classifications have been found to be useful in identifying body types of both males and females. Rarely has an individual been found who would be classified as an extreme type as described above; rather, he would have some combination of characteristics of all three types. There is usually a predominance of characteristics of one classification, however, and this is considered the basic body type. The somatotyping procedure involves rating an individual according to the characteristics he possesses for all three classifications. A rating of from 1 to 7 is given to indicate the degree of characteristics possessed in each classification, with 1 being lowest and 7 being highest. This procedure results in a three-digit rating that describes the body build of that individual. The digits are always written in the order used for presenting the three body types above, i.e. endomorphy, mesomorphy, ectomorphy. A rating of 721 then, would indicate an extreme endomorph, 271 an extreme mesomorph, and 127 an extreme ectomorph.

With a little bit of practice, after becoming familiar with the characteristics associated with the three body types, it should be possible for any of the readers to observe their students and give them a body type rating. As a double check for the subjective rating, you can also compute the ponderal index for each sudent. The ponderal index is found by using this formula: $PI = H/\sqrt[3]{WT}$. By referring to Figure 1, you can calculate the ponderal index by placing a ruler on the appropriate height and weight of an individual and checking the point where it intersects on the ponderal index column. Although the ponderal index is most helpful as an indication of the ectomorph component, it can serve as a rough estimate for all three when used along with a subjective rating. Generally speaking, a ponderal index that falls somewhere between 16.0 and 13.90 corresponds with the ectomorphic body type; one which falls between 13.85 and 11.90 would correspond with a mesomorphic type; between 12.00 and 9.00, it would correspond with the endomorphic type. The preceding categories are given as very rough measures, and it is suggested that if the ponderal index measure does not agree with your subjective rating, you should place more importance on the subjective rating. Sheldon[62] has prepared extensive charts which give the possible somatotype ratings for various ponderal indices, and for those readers who are interested in a more detailed analysis, we suggest that you consult his *Atlas of Men*.

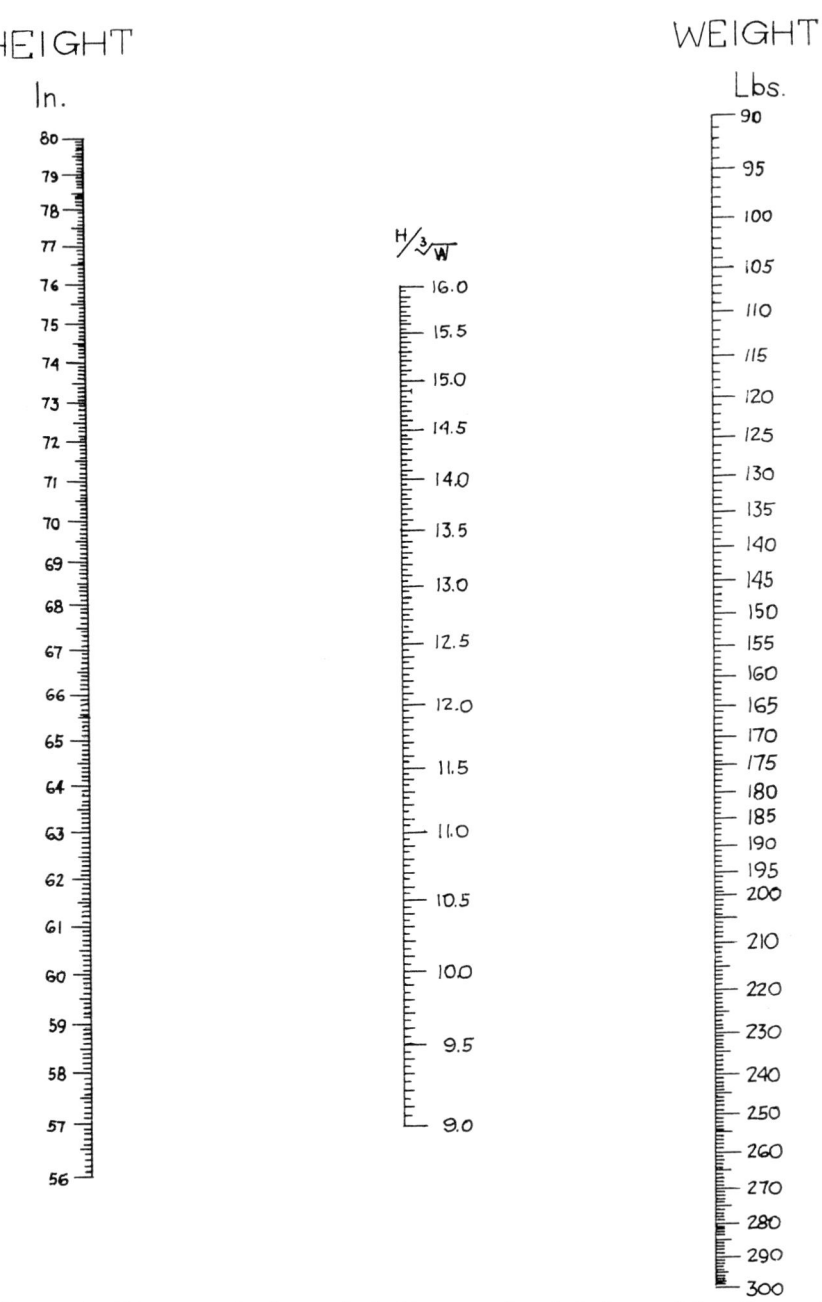

Figure 1. Nomograph for calculating ponderal index. (Courtesy of Willgoose, Carl E.: *Evaluation in Health Education and Physical Education.* New York, McGraw-Hill, 1961.)

When you have determined the basic body type of your students, you can further check your accuracy by consulting other kinds of characteristics which have been shown to be directly associated with body build. Although there have been numerous scales developed, the temperament scale will probably be the most easily observed. The body types with which each characteristic is most often associated are shown in Table II.

TABLE II
SCALE FOR TEMPERAMENT

Endomorph	*Mesomorph*	*Ectomorph*
1. Relaxation in posture and movement	Assertiveness of posture and movement	Restraint in posture and movement tightness
2. Love of physical comfort	Love of physical adventure	Physiological over-response
3. Slow reaction	The energetic characteristic	Overly fast reactions
4. Love of eating	Need and enjoyment of exercise	Love of privacy
5. Pleasure in digestion	Love of risk and chance	Secretiveness of feeling, emotional restraint
6. Love of polite ceremony	Bold directness of manner	Self-conscious motility of eyes and face
7. Indiscriminate amiability	Competitive aggressiveness	Inhibited social address
8. Greed for affection	Psychological callousness	Resistance to habit, poor routinizing
9. Evenness of emotional flow	Ruthlessness, freedom from squeamishness	Unpredictability of attitude
10. Need for people when troubled	Need for action when troubled	Need for solitude when troubled
11. Orientation toward childhood and family relationships	Orientation toward goals and activities of youth	Orientation toward the later periods of life

Courtesy of Willgoose, Carl E.: *Evaluation in Health Education and Physical Education.* New York, McGraw-Hill, 1961.

SELECTED READINGS

For further information in the area of posture measurement, the following are suggested.

1. Clarke, H. Harrison: *Application of Measurement to Health and Physical Education,* 4th ed. Englewood Cliffs, Prentice-Hall, 1967, pp. 414–421.

2. Scott, M. Gladys, and French, Esther: *Measurement and Evaluation in Physical Education.* Dubuque, W. C. Brown, 1959, pp. 123–124.

For further information in the area of anthropometric measurement and body types, see below.

1. Johnson, Barry L., and Nelson, Jack K.: *Practical Measurements for Evaluation in Physical Education.* Minneapolis, Burgess, 1969, pp. 59–76.
2. Willgoose, Carl E.: *Evaluation in Health Education and Physical Education.* New York, McGraw-Hill, 1961, pp. 287–327.

Chapter 4

MEASUREMENT OF PHYSIOLOGICAL EFFICIENCY

> He is not one of a series but a single entity and anything less than unique consideration of the whole man will be something less than adequate.
> —Dr. Charles Sellers

ACCORDING TO SMITH,[67] our unique movement behavior begins with *inherited me* and evolves into a product of the interaction between *me* and my physical-social environment. Consequently, movement is a complex quality and is influenced by many and varied forces. Primarily, the authors feel that those physiological factors which *underlie* the performance of *all* functional movement are cardiovascular efficiency, flexibility, muscular strength and muscular endurance. Other factors considered by the authors to be secondary components of all functional movement are agility, balance, kinesthetic perception, power, reaction time and speed of movement, and rhythm (see Ch. 5). Actually, these factors are not separate components and do not operate as entities in themselves. They are inextricably related and interwoven into our experiences, and eventually, all of these factors must be viewed in relation to the whole individual. The totality and unity of the individual, therefore, is divided into segments only for a better understanding of the factors themselves and the ways in which they can be measured.

CARDIOVASCULAR EFFICIENCY

This term, which is also referred to as circulorespiratory efficiency, means the ability of the person's circulatory and respiratory systems to adjust to and recover from the effects of exercise and work.

Most authorities consider maximal oxygen uptake to be the most valid way to measure this factor. This measurement, which involves the amount of oxygen consumed per kilogram of body weight per minute of exercise, requires expensive equipment and exacting and time-consuming administration and is out of the immediate reach of many schools and colleges. A number of other tests have been devised to measure cardiovascular function. Some of these tests simply require the person to perform a sustained, total body movement, such as running a prescribed distance; the individual's cardiovascular endurance is measured by the elapsed time required to cover the distance. Other tests have sought to determine cardiovascular fitness through pulse rate and blood pressure measurement taken under various conditions which involve changes in the body position, before and after different degrees of work.[37]

One such test that has been developed to measure general efficiency of the body (especially the heart and circulatory system) in adapting to and recovering from hard work is presented in this section along with norms for mentally retarded boys and girls. This test was selected by the authors because it does not require expensive equipment, it is relatively easy to administer and it is a valid measure of cardiovascular efficiency.*

Modified Harvard Step Test
(Skubic Hodgkins Revision [65])

Materials Needed

A stable bench, stool or platform and a watch or clock with a second hand are needed. The height of the bench used for this test varies from thirteen inches to twenty inches, depend-

---

* *Caution:* The authors would like to point out that due to the relatively high incidence of circulatory and respiratory problems with these individuals, *each* person should be subjected to a reasonably thorough physical examination prior to administration of this test. The authors further recommend that additional caution be exercised when administering the test to children with Downs syndrome or to individuals with a history of other kinds of organic dysfunction. If there is any doubt about the physical condition of the individual taking the test, it should be advisable not to force him to exert maximum effort.

ing on the type of individuals being tested. Because of the general physical condition and the incidence of physical handicaps of mentally retarded children, the authors recommend that a thirteen-inch bench be used.

Procedure

The individual stands in front of the bench and on the command, begins to step onto the bench with one foot, then the other; on the third count, he steps down with one foot, then the other (one up—two up—three down—four down). The cadence is twenty-four steps per minute, which means the person being tested will step up with both feet on the bench and bring both feet down to the floor a total of twenty-four times during each minute. The person taking the test should keep his body erect; he may start with either foot and may alternate feet periodically, but he may not jump up or down but must step. The person being tested should attempt to continue stepping for a period of *three minutes,* but may stop at any time he begins to feel tired. A pulse count is taken for thirty seconds following *one minute* of rest whether he remained the three minutes or stopped any time preceding the prescribed limit. As soon as the person ceases stepping, he should be seated and remain quiet for one minute; then the pulse is counted for thirty seconds at the wrist or carotid artery in the neck.

Scoring

The following formula is used for computing the individual's cardiovascular efficiency score:

$$\text{Efficiency score} = \frac{\text{Number of seconds completed} \times 100}{\text{Recovery pulse} \times 5.6}$$

Example: Person tested stepped for two minutes, thirty seconds, and his pulse count for thirty seconds following one minute of rest was sixty.

$$\frac{150 \times 100}{60 \times 5.6} = \frac{15000}{336} = 45$$

Considerations for Assessment

Some considerations for assessment are listed below.

1. A protective padding on the bench is recommended as a precaution for the knee in case the person taking the test stumbles as he steps up and down.

2. Three assistants are recommended for administering the test: one to watch the time and record the precise length of time the person continued stepping; another to check the pulse, and a third to assist the student when necessary (holding the hand or watching the back).

3. A demonstration and several trials should be given before administering the test in order to achieve a good performance. Results will also be better if the test is administered to only one person at a time.

FLEXIBILITY

Flexibility, another factor of functional movement, pertains to the individual's ability to move the body and its parts through a wide range of motion without undue strain to the

TABLE III

PERCENTILE NORMS FOR MODIFIED HARVARD STEP TEST

Boys		Girls	
Percentile	Efficiency Score	Percentile	Efficiency Score
95	95	95	82
90	88	90	80
85	84	85	74
80	80	80	63
75	79	75	56
70	78	70	52
65	77	65	46
60	76	60	45
55	73	55	43
50	72	50	37
45	67	45	33
40	66	40	32
35	60	35	27
30	57	30	25
25	55	25	22
20	38	20	18
15	30	15	17
10	26	10	13
5	17	5	12

Based on the scores of 53 boys and 43 girls (classified as Educable Mentally Retarded) in the Dallas-Ft. Worth-Denton, Texas area.

articulations and muscle attachments. Flexibility measurements include flexion exercises (the angle of the body and its articulations are decreased through movement), and extension exercises (the angle of the body and its articulations are increased through movement).[37] It is presently agreed that lack of adequate flexibility has often been linked with low back pain, a hypokinetic disease.

While there are a number of tests which can be used to assess flexibility of different areas of the body, only two will be presented because of the reasons stated previously. The norms are given only for the first of these tests.

The Modified Sit and Reach Test [37]

Materials Needed

Tape measures or yardsticks are the only materials needed for this test. Several testing stations may be set up and a tape measure or yardstick would be needed for each station.

Figure 2. Modified Sit and Reach Test.

Procedure

The yardstick or tape measure is placed on the floor and secured with masking tape. The individual is seated on the floor in a position with the legs extended and spread on either side of the yardstick and with the heels of both feet in line with the fifteen-inch mark on the yardstick. The performer should bob forward three times, and each time should reach forward with both hands and touch the tape as far out as possible as is shown in Figure 2.

Scoring

Each time the performer bobs forward, measure to the nearest quarter of an inch the farthest point on the tape that is touched with the fingertips. The best of the three trials is recorded as the score.

Considerations for Assessment

In order to measure correctly the flexion of the hip and

TABLE IV
PERCENTILE NORMS FOR THE MODIFIED SIT AND REACH TEST

Boys		Girls	
Percentile	Raw Score	Percentile	Raw Score
95	20.50	95	20.50
90	19.75	90	19.25
85	19.00	85	18.50
80	18.50	80	18.25
75	18.00	75	17.50
70	16.75	70	17.25
65	15.75	65	17.00
60	15.25	60	16.00
55	15.00	55	15.50
50	14.00	50	15.00
45	13.25	45	14.75
40	13.00	40	14.25
35	12.50	35	13.25
30	11.50	30	12.50
25	11.00	25	10.75
20	10.25	20	10.00
15	10.00	15	9.00
10	8.00	10	8.50
5	7.50	5	7.00

Based on the scores of 69 boys and 51 girls (classified as Educable Mentally Retarded) in the Dallas-Hurst-Denton, Texas area.

back, as well as the elasticity of the hamstring muscles, the following considerations are recommended:

1. An assistant should hold the knees of the performer to assure their extension when reaching.
2. Chalk can be used on the fingertips to assist in identifying the farthest point reached on the tape.
3. Assistance should be given the performer by touching his head and shoulders to assure that these body parts are also moving forward.

Wells Sit and Reach Test [77]

This test also measures trunk flexibility and can be used as an alternate to the Modified Sit and Reach Test.

Materials Needed

The equipment consists of a 24" × 28" piece of plywood with lines drawn horizontally at one-half inch intervals. The center line is marked 0; the inch lines above the 0 are numbered 1 through 12, and the lines below 0 are numbered minus 1 through 12. The support for the scale is in the form of a plus sign, made of eleven-inch boards resting on their edges.

Procedure

The performer is seated on the floor with the balls of his feet pressed against the apparatus. The zero line coincides with the rear surface of the crossboard and the minus values are toward the subject. The person reaches forward, palms down, and touches the scale as far out as he possibly can.

Scoring

Three trials are given and the maximum distance reached with the fingertips is recorded as the measure of flexibility. The legs must be kept in a fully extended position as the performer reaches forward.

Considerations for Assessment

Use the same suggestions given for the previous test.

MUSCULAR ENDURANCE

The third factor which underlies our functional movement efficiency concerns the ability of the individual's muscles to repeat identical movements or pressure, or the maintenance of a certain degree of tension in the muscles over a period of time. Muscular endurance may either be *dynamic* or *static*. It should be remembered that muscular endurance is closely associated with strength. While this is true, the measurement of the two factors is different. Muscular endurance scores are based on the number of repetitions executed or the length of time a set tension is maintained, while strength scores are based on the maximum amount of weight lifted or the force exerted.[37]

The following selected tests for both dynamic and static muscular endurance are quite practical for the majority of schools in terms of time, equipment and cost.

Chin-ups (Boys Only)[2]

This measures muscular endurance of the arms and shoulder girdle in pulling the body upward.

Materials Needed

A horizontal bar one and one-half inches in diameter is needed, raised so that the tallest performer cannot touch the ground or floor from a hanging position. A piece of pipe or the rungs of a ladder may be substituted for the standard equipment.

Procedure

The performer places his hands on the bar with the palms facing inward, outward or reversed, depending upon his preference. He then attempts to raise and lower his body as many times as possible, making certain that the chin touches above the bar each time the body is raised and that the body is fully extended each time it is lowered. A hop-up movement and swinging should be avoided (holding the performer stationary could possibly afford a better score). Only one trial is recommended unless the administrator feels the performer could do better on a second trial.

Scoring
The number of completed chin-ups is recorded.

Considerations for Assessment
There are no special considerations to be recommended for this test.

Flexed-Arm Hang (For Girls)[2]
This measures static muscular endurance of the arms and shoulders.

Materials Needed
A horizontal bar is needed, one and one-half inches in diameter and raised so that the tallest performer cannot touch the ground or floor from a hanging position. A piece of pipe or the rungs of a ladder may be substituted for the standard equipment.

Procedure
Using an overhand grasp and with the assistance of two spotters (one in front and one behind), the performer raises the body from the floor so that the chin is above or even with the bar and the elbows are flexed. Time is started as soon as the individual is in the proper flexed hang position and the watch is stopped when the chin drops below the level of the bar or the head is tilted backward.

Scoring
The score is recorded as the number of seconds, to the near-

est second, that the performer maintains the proper body position.

Considerations for Assessment

The following are to be considered:

1. If necessary, a stool may be used to place the performer in the correct position and to assist him in establishing the kinesthetic feeling of the position.

2. Trials should be given preceding the actual testing to assure each performer an opportunity to perform correctly and to the best of his ability.

Sit-ups (Girls and Boys)[37]

These provide a measure of dynamic muscular endurance of the abdominal muscles.

Materials Needed

Any soft surface, preferably a mat, will do.

Procedure

The performer lies on his back with the knees flexed so that the heels are about ten inches from the seat. The fingers are interlaced behind the neck and the sit-ups are executed by alternating the left elbow to a touch of the inside of the right knee and the right elbow to a touch of the inside of the left knee. This exercise is repeated as many times as possible.

Scoring

The score is the maximum number of repetitions performed in an unlimited time.

Considerations for Assessment

Listed below are some considerations.

1. Repetitions are not scored if the fingers are not interlaced behind the head, or when the knees are not touched.

2. The back of the head should touch the mat every time before curling to the sit-up position.

3. An assistant should hold the performer's feet to the floor a few inches apart.

4. If it appears that the performer is unfamiliar with the execution of the sit-up, several trials should be given before starting the test.

Squat Jumps (Girls and Boys)[37]

This is a measure of dynamic muscular endurance of the legs.

Materials Needed

A soft surface, preferably a mat, is needed.

Procedure

The hands are clasped or interlaced behind the top of the head. One foot is a step ahead of the other; then, the performer assumes a squat-down position so that the seat almost touches the rear heel. The performer then jumps upward, extending the legs and switching the position of the feet. The exercise is continued as long as possible without a rest.

Scoring

A point is scored for each correct repetition of the exercise.

Considerations for Assessment

These are listed below.

1. When and if the performer stops to rest, this score is recorded.

2. The performer should be instructed to squat down, *not* drop down, due to possible damage to the ligaments of the knees because of the applied force.

3. Conditioning is recommended preceding this test due to the soreness which can occur in the calves and thighs. Several

trials are also recommended to give the performer the kinesthetic feeling of performing correctly and to the best of his ability.

MUSCULAR STRENGTH

The last factor (and perhaps the most important), considered by the authors to underlie the action of all functional movement is that of muscular strength. The human body has frequently been referred to as a machine, primarily because it is capable of performing mechanical work. It can be thought of as a system of levers that are devices by which mechanical work can be performed. When we speak of strength, we are referring to the amount of force which the muscles can exert in order to perform a certain amount of work. Strength has also been defined as the muscular force exerted against both movable and immovable objects.

Strength is most validly measured by tests which require a single maximum effort of muscular force on a given movement or position. Sometimes the movement or position is one which involves a shortening of the muscle and movement at the particular joint involved, and this is known as *isotonic* or *dynamic* strength. When the muscular force is exerted against an immovable object, we use the term *isometric* or *static* strength. Both types of contractions, isotonic and isometric, will be considered in this section along with the norms for some specific strength tests.

As previously mentioned, strength is considered to involve a single, maximum exertion of muscular force. Many times people think that activities such as push-ups and sit-ups are good tests of muscular strength. It is true that a high correlation exists between muscular strength and muscular endurance, but a task which involves repeated exertions of the muscles is really measuring muscular endurance, not strength per se. One of the difficulties in strength testing, which has contributed to the confusion, is that the best tests for measuring muscular strength involve equipment which is expensive, and the tests are not practical to administer. The authors have chosen a few tests to present in this section which are practical to administer and yet still get a true measure of muscular strength.

Grip Strength (Girls and Boys)
This test measures strength of the hands.

Materials Needed
The grip dynamometer is used to obtain scores for the strength of grip of each hand. This instrument may be purchased from the C. H. Stoelting Company of Chicago, Illinois. A manuometer can also be used to measure grip strength.

Procedure
The dynamometer is first adjusted to fit the size of the person's hand. When the dynamometer is comfortably positioned in the person's hand, he is then instructed to squeeze steadily as hard as he can. The same procedure is then repeated for the opposite hand.

Scoring
Three trials should be given for each hand and the highest score recorded as the grip strength for each hand. The dial of the dynamometer gives the amount of force exerted in kilograms. (One kilogram is equal to 2.2 pounds.) *

Considerations for Assessment
This is a relatively simple test to administer and, after becoming familiar with adjusting and reading the dynamometer, the administrator will not have any problems with it. The only consideration which warrants mention, in terms of testing the mentally retarded child, is that the test administrator should be sure that the student is exerting maximum force. Some of these children lack experience in the exertion of force and may need some added instruction before a score is recorded.

Note: The raw scores on the following norms are in pounds. If the reader uses a dynamometer to measure grip strength, he should first convert the raw scores to pounds before using the tables.

TABLE V
PERCENTILE NORMS FOR GRIP STRENGTH OF THE LEFT HAND

Boys		Girls	
Percentile	Raw Score	Percentile	Raw Score
95	119	95	76
90	106	90	74
85	101	85	64
80	99	80	62
75	96	75	61
70	93	70	60
65	88	65	59
60	81	60	57
55	78	55	55
50	74	50	52
45	69	45	50
40	65	40	49
35	62	35	47
30	60	30	45
25	58	25	43
20	52	20	41
15	49	15	39
10	44	10	33
5	37	5	31

Based on the scores of 72 boys and 50 girls (classified as Educable Mentally Retarded) in the Dallas-Hurst-Denton, Texas area.

TABLE VI
PERCENTILE NORMS FOR GRIP STRENGTH OF THE RIGHT HAND

Boys		Girls	
Percentile	Raw Score	Percentile	Raw Score
95	140	95	77
90	118	90	75
85	110	85	71
80	103	80	66
75	101	75	63
70	99	70	62
65	92	65	60
60	89	60	58
55	84	55	56
50	82	50	54
45	77	45	52
40	75	40	51
35	72	35	50
30	69	30	47
25	66	25	44
20	61	20	42
15	59	15	40
10	51	10	38
5	41	5	33

Based on the scores of 72 boys and 51 girls (classified as Educable Mentally Retarded) in the Dallas-Hurst-Denton, Texas area.

Spring Scale Measurement [37]

A very important body area for both strength measurement and strength development is that of the upper arms and shoulders. Many of the everyday tasks of living require a pulling or pushing movement which involves the muscles in these areas of the body. The two tests which are recommended for use with this equipment, and for which norms are given, are the Curl and Press.

Materials Needed

All of the equipment needed for constructing the spring-scale device are available at most hardware stores and the total cost is approximately $15. The necessary items for the device are as follow:

1. One 160-pound spring scale.
2. Two heavy duty eye hooks.
3. Two chain links.
4. Two eighteen-inch chain sections.
5. One five-foot chain section.
6. Two "S" hooks.
7. One screw hook.
8. One wooden bar (two-foot length of hickory).
9. One piece of wood approximately two feet wide and four to six feet long and two inches high.

Procedure

The procedure is described below.

1. Curl: Have the performer stand on the wooden platform with feet spaced shoulder-width apart. Position the person's arms so that the elbows are close to the body, the lower arms are extended at waist-level to form a 90° angle and the palms are facing up. Place the wooden bar in the performer's hands and attach the chain at the appropriate distance. Instruct the person to keep his back and legs straight and his feet on the platform and, using only the arms, to pull up as hard as possible (see Fig. 3).

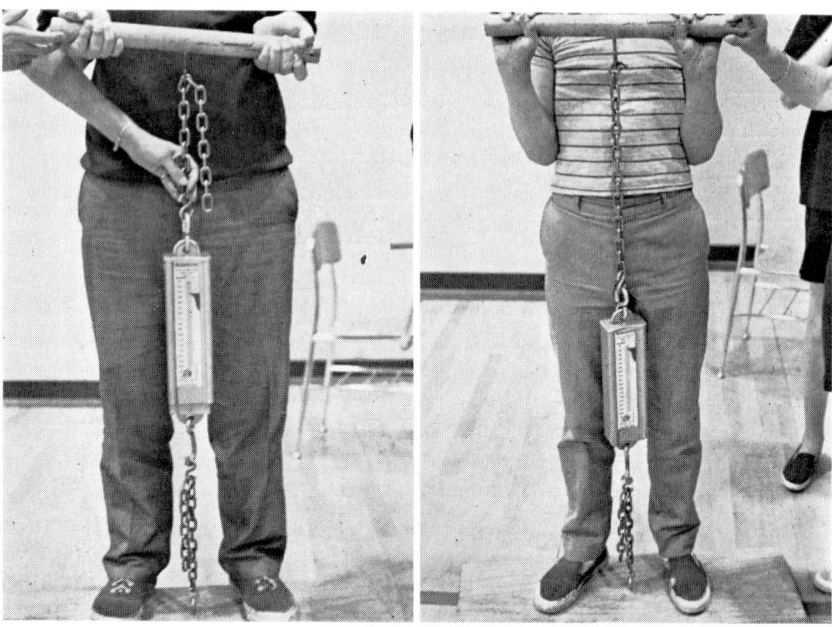

Figure 3. Spring Scale Curl Test.

Figure 4. Spring Scale Press Test.

2. Press: Have the student stand on the wooden platform with the feet spaced shoulder-width apart. Position the person's arms so that the hands are raised to a point even with the eyes and the palms are facing up. Place the wooden bar in the performer's hands and attach the chain at the appropriate distance. Instruct the person to keep the back and legs straight, feet flat on the platform, and to push the bar up using only the arms (see Fig. 4).

Scoring

The test administrator should keep his eyes on the level of the scale and watch until the needle reaches the greatest number of pounds, with a steady pull or push. Two trials are given and the higher of the two is recorded. (This scoring procedure applies to both the Curl and Press.)

Considerations for Assessment

Some considerations are as listed below.

1. Many mentally retarded children have difficulty with the kinesthetic feeling of applying force. In order to assure reliable scores, then, it is advisable to give them an opportunity to become acquainted with the testing device several days prior to testing.

2. It is very important that the described body position (legs and back straight) be maintained during testing. For this reason, it is suggested that two people be used to administer the tests. One person can watch to make sure there is no force being applied except with the arms and shoulders, and the other can watch the needle on the scale.

3. Since the spring scale has just one needle, the dial must be watched very carefully in order to notice when the maximum amount of pull is registered.

TABLE VII
PERCENTILE NORMS FOR SPRING SCALE PRESS TEST

Boys		Girls	
Percentile	*Raw Score*	*Percentile*	*Raw Score*
95	141	95	90
90	135	90	82
85	130	85	74
80	125	80	68
75	119	75	64
70	114	70	61
65	106	65	57
60	102	60	55
55	100	55	51
50	94	50	46
45	90	45	43
40	85	40	41
35	77	35	40
30	74	30	36
25	64	25	35
20	60	20	31
15	54	15	28
10	40	10	24
5	29	5	15

Based on the scores of 69 boys and 52 girls (classified as Educable Mentally Retarded) in the Dallas-Hurst-Denton, Texas area.

TABLE VIII
PERCENTILE NORMS FOR SPRING SCALE CURL TEST

Boys		Girls	
Percentile	Raw Score	Percentile	Raw Score
95	110	95	67
90	105	90	58
85	96	85	52
80	91	80	46
75	88	75	45
70	85	70	44
65	81	65	42
60	78	60	41
55	75	55	40
50	72	50	39
45	70	45	36
40	66	40	34
35	64	35	33
30	60	30	32
25	57	25	31
20	51	20	30
15	44	15	26
10	32	10	25
5	21	5	22

Based on the scores of 70 boys and 39 girls (classified as Educable Mentally Retarded) in the Dallas-Hurst-Denton, Texas area.

As mentioned previously, the tests presented in this chapter to measure the four primary components of movement efficiency were chosen besause they are practical to administer, yet are still valid measures of the factors. The references included in the "Selected Readings" will give information about many other tests that are available.

This chapter has dealt with the diagnosing of strengths and weaknesses in the areas of cardiovascular efficiency, flexibility, muscular strength and muscular endurance. In later chapters, you will find appropriate activities to be used for developing these areas.

SELECTED READINGS

1. Clarke, H. Harrison: *Muscular Strength and Endurance in Man.* Englewood Cliffs, Prentice-Hall, 1966.
2. Corbin, Charles B., Dowell, Linus J., and Landiss, Carl W.: *Concepts and Experiments in Physical Education.* Dubuque, W. C. Brown, 1968.
3. Cratty, Bryant J.: *Motor Activity and the Education of Retardates.* Philadelphia, Lea & Febiger, 1969.

4. de Vries, Herbert A.: *Physiology of Exercise.* Dubuque, W. C. Brown, 1966.
5. Johnson, Barry L., and Nelson, Jack K.: *Practical Measurements for Evaluation in Physical Education.* Minneapolis, Burgess, 1969.
6. Mathews, Donald K.: *Measurement in Physical Education.* Philadelphia, Saunders, 1968.

Chapter 5

MEASUREMENT OF FACTORS IMPORTANT IN COMPLEX MOTOR PERFORMANCE

It is the happy constitution of the body which renders the operations of the mind facile and sure.
—Rousseau

MOVEMENT EFFICIENCY depends primarily upon a good foundation composed of muscular strength, muscular and cardiovascular endurance and flexibility. With this foundation, the individual is equipped to handle the everyday tasks of living and to perform certain basic motor patterns and skills. Efficient movement, necessary for dealing with more complex motor tasks, involves additional factors which must be evaluated and developed. Motor tasks which require rapid movement of the body or its segments, quick starts and stops, or focusing upon an external object while moving or responding quickly to a stimulus, require a certain degree of such factors as agility, power, reaction time, balance, kinesthetic perception and speed of movement. In order to gain an understanding of the total capacity of an individual for motor performance and to thus plan an appropriate program for developing his movement efficiency, it is necessary to evaluate these additional factors.

AGILITY

This factor involves the ability of an individual to rapidly change body position and direction in a precise manner. Selected tests of agility, which are practical in terms of time, equipment, cost and ease of administration, are described below.

Burpee Test (Squat Thrust)*

This is a test which measures the individual's ability to rapidly change body position.

Materials Needed

A watch or clock with a second hand is needed.

Procedure

Start from a standing position, bend the knees and bend at the waist and place the hands on the floor in front of the feet; thrust the legs back as far as possible, resting the body on the hands and feet; return to the second or squat position; then rise to the standing position. On the signal "Go," these movements are repeated as quickly as possible until the "Stop" signal is given.

Scoring

The score is the number of parts executed in ten seconds.

Example: Squatting and placing the hands on the floor is *one*, thrusting the legs to the rear is *two*, returning to a squat-rest position is *three*, and returning to the standing position is *four*.

Considerations for Assessment

Listed below are some considerations for assessment.

1. A number of trials and demonstrations should be given preceding the day on which the test is administered.

2. *Individual testing* is recommended unless assistance can be provided for counting the movements of each person being tested.

3. Instruct the individual to keep the weight over the hands and to curl the toes under when thrusting the legs backward.

4. Coordination of the movements involved may prove dif-

---

* To the best of the author's knowledge, the Squat Thrust was first presented as a test by Royal H. Burpee.

ficult for many of the individuals to be tested, and prior instruction will be helpful. To hasten acquisition of the squat position, instruct the individual to slowly bend to the floor from standing position with the arms to the side and then proceed with thrusting of the legs.

Side Step Test [37]

This measures the rapidity with which the individual can move the body laterally and make changes of movement to the opposite direction.

Materials Needed

A watch or clock with a second hand and *colored* tape are needed.

Procedure

Start from a standing position astride the center line (see Fig. 5). On the signal "Go," the individual sidesteps or slides to the right until his foot has touched or crossed the line; then he sidesteps or slides to the left until his left foot has touched or crossed the outside line on the left side. These lateral movements are repeated as rapidly as possible for a period of ten seconds.

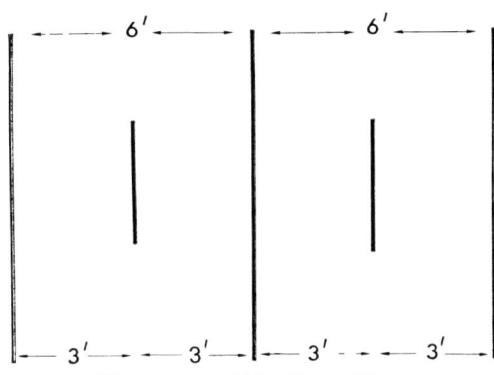

Figure 5. Side Step Test.

Scoring

A one-foot tick mark should be placed between the center line and each outside line. A point is scored each time the individual crosses a marker from the center line. For example, moving to the right, the person crosses the tick mark for *one*, the outside marker for *two*, back across the tick mark for *three*, across the center marker for *four*, across the left tick mark for *five*, across the outside marker for *six*, and so on until the ten seconds have elapsed.

Considerations for Assessment

Some considerations for assessment follow:

1. It is incorrect to cross one foot over the other. If the movement is not a distinct slide, *do not score* the point.
2. Many trials should be given prior to administration of the test.
3. When demonstrating, have the individual imitate the director from a position behind him and this will assist the student in acquiring the movement more quickly.
4. The footwear of the person being tested is an important factor in performance on this test. If the test administrator feels that the shoes being worn will not provide a good grip or footing, it is suggested that the individual perform barefooted.

Quadrant Jump [37]

This test measures the ability of the individual to change body position rapidly by jumping.

Materials Needed

A watch or clock with a second hand and colored tape or chalk.

Procedure

The individual starts behind the starting tick mark and jumps with both feet into Area 1, Area 2, Area 3 and Area 4 in that order, and then back to Area 1 (see Fig. 6). These

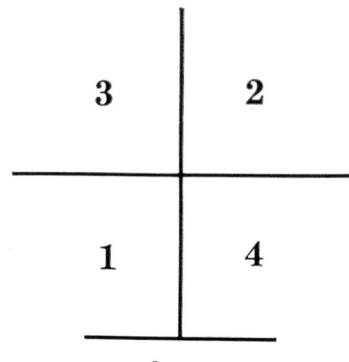

Figure 6. Quadrant Jump Test.

movements, in the order described above, are continued until the signal "Stop" is given after ten seconds have elapsed.

Scoring

The score for each individual is the number of times the feet land in a correct zone in the ten-second time period. The best score of two trials is recorded.

Considerations for Assessment

These are as follow:

1. Again, sufficient practice and demonstration should be provided before administering this test. Particularly important is making sure that the people to be tested understand the sequence of the areas to be jumped into and that they understand that they must jump and land with both feet together.

2. A point is *not* scored if the feet or a foot lands on a line, or if the jump is into the wrong zone.

3. One assistant should be used to count the number of jumps and a second assistant to count the errors made.

BALANCE

Evidence appears to indicate that good balance depends upon the interaction of two primary systems, (1) the muscular feedback from the postural muscles which control the ability to maintain an upright postion, and (2) the visual system which aids the individual to "tie himself down" to gravity when a variable has been imposed on him to create disequilibrium.[19] The two types of balance tests commonly used are those which measure *static* balance and those which measure *dynamic* balance. *Static balance* is generally defined as the physical ability of an individual which enables him to hold a stationary position, and *dynamic balance* is the ability to maintain balance during fairly vigorous movement such as walking railroad tracks (Johnson and Nelson[37]).

Nelson Balance Test [37]

This measures both static and dynamic balance in a single test.

Materials Needed

Nine small wooden blocks ($2'' \times 4'' \times 8''$), four of which are painted red, are required. A ten-foot wooden balance beam, held edgewise by three triangular-shaped supports; a stop-

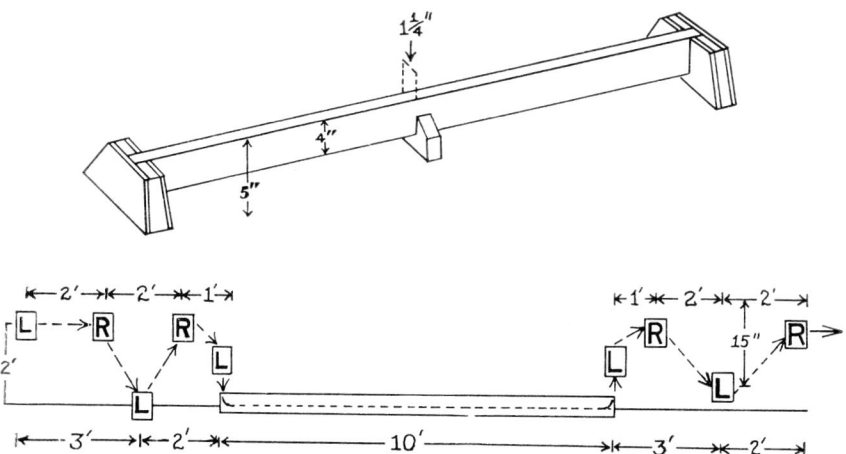

Figure 7. Nelson Balance Test. (Courtesy of Johnson, Barry L., and Nelson, Jack K.: *Practical Measurements for Evaluation in Physical Education.* Minneapolis, Burgess, 1969.)

watch, tape measure and chalk or tape to mark the position of the blocks on the floor are also needed. (See Fig. 7 for dimensions and position of the blocks and beam.)

Procedure

When the individual is ready, he steps onto the first block on the ball of the left foot and holds the right foot up off the floor, at which time the test administrator starts the watch and counts aloud "1-2-3-4-5" to signify five seconds. At the end of five seconds, the individual proceeds along the path, leaping from one block to the other and alternating feet each time. Each time he steps onto one of the *red* blocks he must hold the stationary position with the other foot up while the tester counts aloud the five seconds. The testee should attempt to move as fast as possible from one block to the other and should leave the red blocks as soon as the count of five is given. He cannot run or leap across the beam, but he should walk heel-to-toe as fast as possible.

Scoring

The score is the total time which elapses from the start of the watch on the first block until the person steps off the last block. Three trials are given and the best of the three is recorded as the score.

Considerations for Assessment

Listed below are some considerations for assessment.

1. Before administering this test, a reasonable amount of time should be spent in acquainting the children with the details of the test and in allowing them to move through the various stages. A demonstration, in which the child is allowed to imitate the leader will be necessary. With some children, it will be necessary to lend assistance by placing the foot in the center of the blocks and by moving the correct leg as they move from one block to the next.

2. Any time the individual's foot touches the floor, he must

Measurement of Motor Performance

get back onto the block at the place where he fell off and proceed from there. The same is true for the balance beam.

3. If the individual leaves one of the "hold" blocks before the five seconds have elapsed, he must return and "hold" for the remaining seconds.

4. If an assistant is available, it will be helpful to have him use a second stopwatch to call the "1-2-3-4-5" seconds on the "hold" blocks.

TABLE IX
PERCENTILE NORMS FOR THE NELSON BALANCE TEST

Boys		Girls	
Percentile	Raw Score	Percentile	Raw Score
95	26.6	95	28
90	27.2	90	30
85	27.8	85	32
80	28.4	80	33
75	29.1	75	34
70	29.8	70	35
65	30.6	65	39
60	31.4	60	41
55	32.4	55	42
50	33.6	50	44
45	35.3	45	55
40	37.3	40	60
35	40.0	35	63
30	42.6	30	65
25	45.0	25	67
20	51.0	20	70
15	64.0	15	82
10	84.0	10	104
5	94.0	5	134

Based on the scores of 60 boys and 40 girls (classified as Educable Mentally Retarded) in the Dallas-Hurst-Denton, Texas area.

KINESTHETIC PERCEPTION

When an individual engages in movement of any kind, there is a continuous flow of sensory information concerning the results of the movement as it progresses. This interval system of feedback about movement and the position of the body is referred to as proprioception. The mechanism of proprioception involves both vestibular and kinesthetic receptors. The vestibular receptors are located in the labyrinths of the inner ear and the kinesthetic receptors are found in (1) the muscle spindle, (2) the Golgi tendon organ, (3) the pacinian corpuscle, and (4) free nerve endings. All of these receptors give the individual a *muscle sense*, which enables him to be aware of the action of his limbs or body segments without having to rely on his visual sense.[21]

Although proprioception is a vital aspect of motor behavior and skilled motor performance, Steinhaus[73] accentuated its importance in all aspects of human behavior when he said:

> We can live without eyes, we can live without ears and would probably sometimes be happier without the sense of smell; but without the messages that come to us from our muscles and joint structures we could not talk, walk, breathe, find our mouth to feed it, or follow the printed line while reading; and probably could not think.

Although the significance of the kinesthetic sense in the learning of many kinds of tasks is readily accepted, this sixth sense presents more difficulty than its five siblings when it comes to measurement. At the present time, no one test has been found which can validly determine an overall or total kinesthetic perceptual ability. There are many tests which have been devised to measure the kinesthetic perception of various parts of the body or of various applications of force in certain muscle groups. The authors have chosen three tests which they feel are most pertinent to the kinesthetic perceptual ability of mentally retarded children.

Horizontal Linear Space Test [80]

This measures the kinesthetic ability to determine a specific position of the arm along a horizontal line.

Materials Needed

A yardstick, measuring tape and blindfold are needed.

Procedure

Tape the yardstick or measuring tape to a wall in front of the seated individual so that it is approximately at eye level for that person (see Fig. 8). The person is instructed to look at the eighteen-inch mark on the stick or tape, point to it with the finger of the dominant hand, and try to sense the position of the arm. Without a practice trial, the individual is then instructed to point to the mark again while blindfolded.

Scoring

The deviation from the desired mark is recorded to the nearest quarter of an inch for each of three trials. The deviations for all three trials are then totaled for the score.

Vertical Linear Space Test [80]

This test measures the kinesthetic ability to determine a specific position of the arm along a vertical line.

Materials Needed

A yardstick, measuring tape and blindfold are needed.

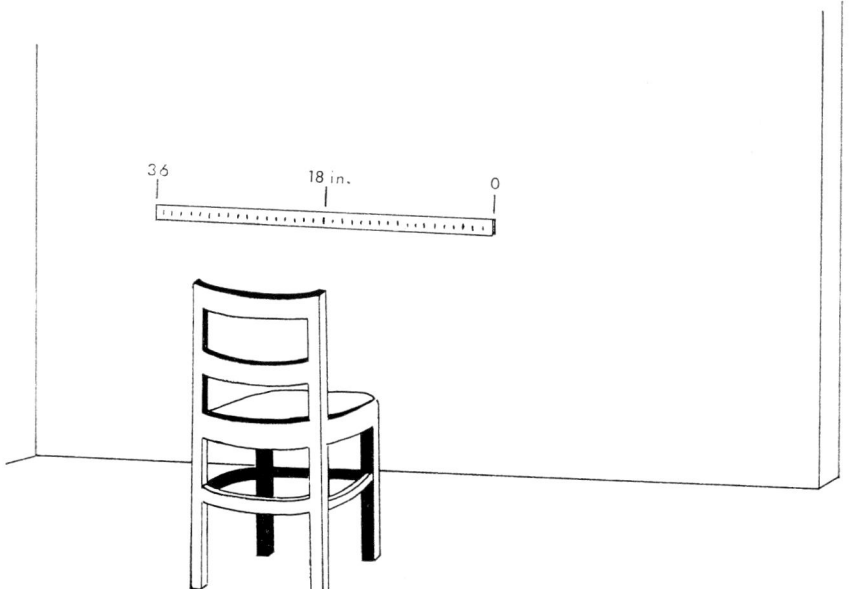

Figure 8. Horizontal Linear Space Test.

TABLE X
PERCENTILE NORMS FOR THE HORIZONTAL LINEAR SPACE TEST

Boys Percentile	Raw Score	Girls Percentile	Raw Score
95	.25	95	.50
90	.50	90	.75
85	.75	85	1.00
80	1.00	80	1.25
75	1.25	75	1.50
70	1.50	70	1.75
65	1.75	65	2.00
60	2.00	60	2.50
55	2.25	55	3.00
50	2.50	50	3.25
45	2.75	45	4.00
40	3.00	40	4.50
35	3.25	35	4.75
30	3.50	30	5.00
25	3.75	25	5.50
20	5.00	20	6.00
15	5.50	15	7.50
10	6.00	10	8.00
5	8.00	5	11.00

Based on the scores of 69 boys and 52 girls (classified as Educable Mentally Retarded) in the Dallas-Hurst-Denton, Texas area.

Procedure

Tape the yardstick or measuring tape vertically to a wall in front of the seated individual so that the sixteen-inch mark is at eye level for each person (see Fig. 9). The individual is instructed to look at the sixteen-inch mark, point to it and try to sense the position of the arm. Without a practice trial, the person is blindfolded and instructed to point to the mark again.

Scoring

The deviation from the desired mark is recorded to the nearest quarter of an inch for each of three trials. The deviations for all three trials are then totaled for the score.

Modified Test of Horizontal and Vertical Linear Space

The separate horizontal and vertical tests were presented because norms are available for them, but the authors have devised a modified version which we feel has certain advan-

Measurement of Motor Performance 71

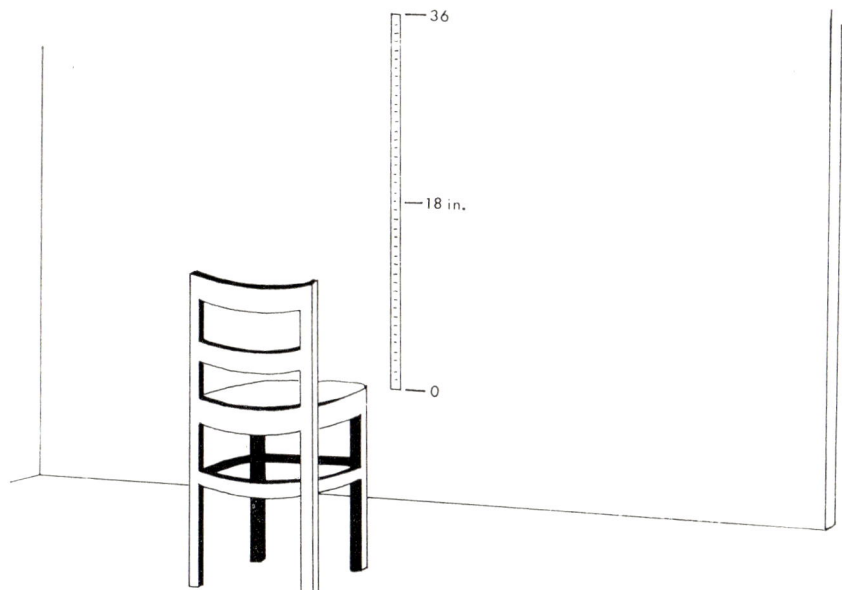

Figure 9. Vertical Linear Space Test.

TABLE XI
PERCENTILE NORMS FOR THE VERTICAL LINEAR SPACE TEST

Boys		Girls	
Percentile	Raw Score	Percentile	Raw Score
95	.75	95	.25
90	1.00	90	.50
85	1.25	85	.75
80	1.50	80	1.00
75	1.75	75	1.25
70	2.00	70	1.50
65	2.25	65	1.75
60	2.50	60	2.00
55	2.75	55	2.25
50	3.00	50	2.50
45	3.25	45	2.75
40	3.50	40	3.00
35	3.75	35	3.25
30	4.00	30	3.50
25	4.25	25	4.00
20	4.50	20	5.75
15	5.00	15	8.25
10	6.00	10	8.50
5	9.00	5	11.50

Based on the scores of 70 boys and 52 girls (classified as Educable Mentally Retarded) in the Dallas-Hurst-Denton, Texas area.

72   The Mentally Retarded Child and His Motor Behavior

tages over the other two and some of the readers might want to use it.

Materials Needed

Instead of using a yardstick or measuring tape, draw the facsimile of a yardstick in both the vertical and horizontal positions on a large piece of paper or cardboard as shown in Figure 10.

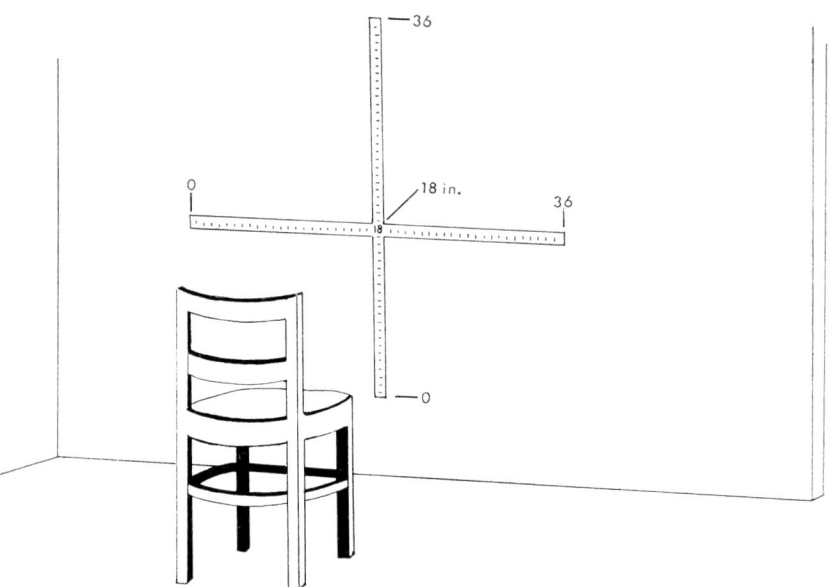

Figure 10. Modified Test of Horizontal and Vertical Linear Space.

Procedure

The chart is placed on the wall in front of the seated individual so that the eighteen-inch mark is at eye level. The person is instructed to point to the eighteen-inch mark, look at it and try to sense the position of the arm. The individual is then blindfolded and instructed to point to the same spot again.

Scoring

Three trials are given, and on each trial the deviations in both the vertical and horizontal positions are recorded. All deviations in the vertical plane are then totaled and all deviations in the horizontal plane totaled as in the preceding tests.

Distance Perception Jump [61]

This determines the ability of an individual to perceive distance by concentrating on the effort involved in a jump.

Materials Needed

Needed are a yardstick or tape measure, blindfold material and chalk or marking tape (see Fig. 11).

Figure 11. Distance Perception Jump.

Procedure

The individual is instructed to *sense* or make an attempt to sense (feel) the distance between the two lines without a practice trial. The person is then blindfolded and instructed to jump from behind one line toward the other line, trying to land with the heels as close to the line as possible.

Scoring

The number of inches, measured to the nearest quarter of an inch, between the heels and the target line is recorded for each of two trials. The total of the two trials is the score. When the heels are not even, measure to or from the heel that is furthest from the target line.

Considerations for Assessment

It is suggested that the person be allowed to see where he lands on the first trial.

POWER

Muscular power involves the ability to release maximum force in the fastest possible time against a resistance in a minimum of time.[37] Pure muscular power is difficult to measure, because it requires the computation of work, in the mechanical sense, done by specific muscle groups. For purposes of evaluating movement efficiency, it is both practical and adequate to use the type of measurement which is known as *athletic power*. This type of measurement is expressed in terms of the distance through which the body or an object is propelled through space.

Standing Broad Jump [2]

The test measures athletic power of the legs in jumping forward.

Materials Needed

Either a mat or the floor may be used. Tape or chalk is

Measurement of Motor Performance

needed for the starting line, along with a tape measure to mark off increments of distance along the landing area.

Procedure

The individual stands behind the starting mark, feet parallel, knees bent and arms back. He then swings the arms forward and at the same time jumps forward as far as possible.

Scoring

The number of inches between the starting line and the nearest heel upon landing is recorded. Three trials are permitted and the best of the three is counted as the score.

Considerations for Assessment

Some considerations are listed below.

1. If the individual falls backward upon landing, measure from the starting line to the nearest part of the body touching the landing surface.
2. Let the children practice the jump until the movement can be executed correctly.

Two-Hand Medicine Ball Put [37]

This measures athletic power of the arms and shoulder girdle.

Materials Needed

Either a four- or six-pound medicine ball, chalk or tape, a small rope, a chair and a tape measure are needed.

Procedure

From a sitting position in a straight-backed chair, the individual holds the ball in both hands with the ball drawn back against the chest and just under the chin. The person then pushes the ball upward and outward for maximum distance. The rope is placed around the individual's chest and held taut to the rear by a partner in order to eliminate a rocking action during the push. The individual's effort should be primarily with the arms.

Scoring

The distance between the spot where the ball lands and the front edge of the chair is recorded for three trials, and the best of the three is counted as the score. One practice trial is given before scoring.

REACTION TIME AND SPEED OF MOVEMENT

Complex motor performance, particularly the type required for many sports activities, is influenced to a large degree by the ability of an individual to react quickly to various stimuli and to make a motor response with speed. *Reaction time* is usually considered to be the amount of time which elapses from the presentation of a stimulus until the response is initiated. *Speed of movement* is considered as the rate at which a person can move his body or parts of his body through space. Although these are complex factors of motor performance, the authors feel that a simple measure of reaction time and speed of hand movement can be useful in assessing the movement efficiency of mentally retarded children.

The Nelson Hand Reaction Test [53]

The test measures simple reaction time of the hand.

Materials Needed

The Nelson Reaction Timer,* a desk or table and a chair are required.

Procedure

Have the individual sit in a chair with the hand and forearm of the dominant hand resting on a table or desk, as shown in

---

* Can be purchased from Fred B. Nelson, P.O. Box 51987, Lafayette, Louisiana (less than $5).

Measurement of Motor Performance 77

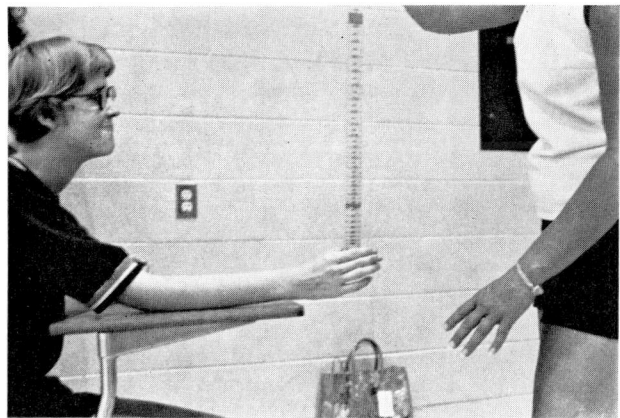

Figure 12. Nelson Reaction Time Test.

Figure 12. The hand should be placed so that the fingers extend beyond the edge of the table about three or four inches. The thumb and index fingers should be about one inch apart, with the upper edges in a horizontal position. The tester holds the stick-timer near the top and lets it hang between the thumb and index finger of the person being tested. The *baseline* of the stick should be even with the upper surface of the individual's thumb. The individual is instructed to watch the black-shaded area of the stick and to react quickly by pinching the thumb and index finger together to catch the stick when it is released. Ten trials are given and each trial should be preceded by the command, "Ready."

Scoring

Each time the person catches the stick, the score is read just above the top of the thumb. The two highest trials and two lowest are discarded and the middle six scores are averaged for the final reaction time score.

Considerations for Assessment

Below are some considerations for assessment.

1. Enough trials should be given to familiarize the individual with the test.

78 *The Mentally Retarded Child and His Motor Behavior*

2. Care should be taken to maintain the proper position of the hands and fingers. After the first several trials, the individual will tend to close the distance between the thumb and forefinger on the reaction test, or in some cases to spread them too far apart.

3. In addition to giving the command of ready, the tester should also observe the readiness of the person before starting the next trial. Some of the mentally retarded children tend to lose their concentration between the trials.

TABLE XII
PERCENTILE NORMS FOR THE NELSON HAND REACTION TEST

Boys		Girls	
Percentile	Raw Score	Percentile	Raw Score
95	.164	95	.161
90	.168	90	.171
85	.179	85	.196
80	.185	80	.199
75	.188	75	.206
70	.191	70	.217
65	.195	65	.221
60	.199	60	.227
55	.201	55	.230
50	.211	50	.236
45	.220	45	.238
40	.229	40	.242
35	.233	35	.245
30	.247	30	.254
25	.255	25	.265
20	.262	20	.273
15	.271	15	.281
10	.280	10	.293
5	.308	5	.307

Based on the scores of 71 boys and 47 girls (classified as Educable Mentally Retarded) in the Dallas-Hurst-Denton, Texas area.

The Nelson Speed of Movement Test [53]

This measures combined reaction and speed of movement of the hands.

Materials Needed

The materials are the same as for the reaction test.

Procedure

The person being tested is seated with his hands resting on the edge of a table. The palms of the hands are facing one another and the lower edge of the little finger is placed on two lines marked on the edge of the table twelve inches apart. The tester holds the stick-timer near its top so that it hangs between the person's palms. The baseline of the stick should be level with the upper edge of the person's thumbs. A preliminary command of "Ready" is given, and as the stick is dropped, the person moves his hands together as quickly as possible to try to catch the stick. The hands may not be moved up or down, but must slide along the surface of the table. Ten trials are given.

Scoring

The timer is read the same way and the average score computed in the same manner as described in the Reaction Test.

Considerations for Assessment

The same suggestions given for the Reaction Test are applicable for the Speed of Movement Test.

Chapter 6

MEASUREMENT OF PERCEPTUAL-MOTOR FUNCTIONING

> Knowledge begins not with "I think therefore I am," but with "I sense therefore I am."
>
> —KEEN

THE AUTHORS' VIEWPOINTS concerning perception parallel that of the present-day thinking of many psychologists. This view is to consider the physical world as our *stimulus*, its effects upon us as *sensation*, and our interpretation of its effects as *perception*. The term "perceptual motor" is being used to describe those functions of the human organism which have a voluntary motor component that depends on sensory perception previous to the motor act and on some kind of sensory feedback.[16]

Our objective for this chapter is to present the procedure for evaluating what we consider to be the foundational components for all learning. In order to appreciate the importance of each of these components, it is helpful to briefly review the process by which we develop the capacity for learning.

Bell has suggested that the main function of the central nervous system is the integration of sensory information for a coordinated motor response.[8] Before the integration can occur, however, there must be present a *willingness* to accomplish an act, a *knowledge* of the internal and external environment and certain *inherent movement patterns* such as reflexes and walking. All three of these elements become particularly significant when one is dealing with learning experiences for young people with educational difficulties. The mentally retarded child will quite frequently exhibit an *unwill-*

ingness to accomplish certain tasks. Although this may stem from a variety of reasons, the important thing to remember is that he must be motivated strongly to perform. Many times the inability to accomplish a given task by the mentally retarded child is interpreted as being the lack of capacity to accomplish while actually, it is simply the lack of motivation or desire to do it. Bell[8] has pointed out that the activity of the reticular formation, located in the brain stem, can be set so that it permits only certain kinds of information to reach the cortex. This neurophysiological phenomenon provides the avenue for us to effectively utilize motivational devices to enhance the perception of sensory information by the learner. The second element necessary for integration is knowledge of the internal and external environment. Piaget[56] reminds us that in the adult, cognitive operations are the end result of a long period of development which involves the internalization of a full behavioral sequence of activities involved in repeatedly coping with or exploring our environment. For many mentally retarded children, this period of development is riddled with interruptions which have prevented the internalization of a full behavioral sequence. For a large percentage of these children, the interruptions result from inadequate sensory perception which can be due to a variety of causes. It is with these various causes, however, that we should be most concerned and to which we will devote most of this chapter. Certain inherent movement patterns, which was the third element necessary for integration, will also be inadequate in many mentally retarded children.

Bruner et al.[13] has noted that, "When the child cannot exhibit the motoric acting out of responses, he cannot organize a central pattern sufficient for language . . . ." This same viewpoint has also been expressed by other authorities, and in our opinion it forms the basis for an understanding of the educational difficulties experienced by many children.

When we have a lamp which fails to illuminate, we might summon an electrician who would start at the initial source, and step by step, examine the circuit to determine where the flaw is. The same sort of procedure is necessary for examining the perceptual circuits of the mentally retarded child. A large part of his inadequate cognitive functioning may result from some interruption in the sensori-perceptual-motor development stages that proceed without pause in the more normal individual. The sequential examination which the authors feel will reveal the most valuable information about a child includes these phases of sensori-perceptual-motor development: (1) body-image, (2) laterality, (3) directionality, (4) temporal-spatial relationships, and (5) sensory efficiency.

BODY-IMAGE

According to Bruner et al.,[13] the body-image is not of importance per se; its primary importance derives from its role in the development of intelligence. He stated that ". . . at first the child's world is known to him principally by the habitual actions he uses for coping with it." This first stage could be termed "body-image intelligence," and is frequently termed "sensori-motor intelligence." From the very beginning of his exploratory quest for knowledge, the individual begins to receive environmental information which must be dealt with in relative rather than absolute terms. It is most essential that he have some point of reference around which to deal with these impressions so that he will be able to compose them into an orderly semblance and thus build a meaningful totality. That point of reference is the individual's own body.

The building of a body-image is a process which occurs for most of us so naturally that we seldom give it a thought. When one is dealing with an individual for whom it has not occurred naturally, however, a knowledge of the building process takes on significance. From the earliest moments of life, and perhaps even before, we begin to receive a variety of sensations which continually mold together into a mental picture that depicts the image of the body to us. There are tactile sensations from the body's surface which constantly transmit impressions of temperature, pain and texture. From the muscle spindles and tendons, we continually receive kinesthetic messages about our state of relaxation, tension and movement. Our internal organs constantly keep us abreast with physiological sensations. In the course of normal development, this continuous barrage of sensations from our own somatic telegraph becomes welded into a *body-image* which later serves as our reference point for all future spatial relationships with the external environment.

For some individuals, the building of the body-image does not occur as described, and Schilder[60] has pointed out the result by saying that "When the knowledge of our own body is incomplete and faulty, all actions for which this knowledge is necessary will be faulty, too."

Body-Image Test [39]

The following test is presented for use in determining the degree to which an individual has developed a body-image. The first part of the test involves the identification of various body parts with the eyes open and is a slight modification of a test developed by Kephart.[39] The authors have added an additional part to the test which involves the same identification with the eyes closed. We believe that a firmly established body-image would include an awareness of body parts through the kinesthetic sense as well as the visual.

Materials Needed

A checklist of test items is needed.

Procedure

Ask the individual to stand facing you at a distance where he will be easily visible. Explain that you are going to give him a series of commands and that after you have given each one, he is to respond by doing what you asked.

Verbal Commands

A. Eyes open

    1. Touch your shoulders.

2. Touch your thighs.
3. Touch your head.
4. Touch your ankles.
5. Touch your ears.
6. Touch your feet.
7. Touch your eyes.
8. Touch your elbows.
9. Touch your knees.
10. Touch your mouth.
11. Touch your back.
12. Touch your stomach.
13. Touch your chest.

B. Eyes closed or blindfolded

Repeat all thirteen items.

Specific Qualities of Performance to Be Observed
Observe for the following:

1. There is hesitancy in any response.
2. The child is decisive in obeying each command.
3. In the paired parts of the body, he touches both members of the pair.
4. When moving toward a part, does the child move accurately to that part or does he start in the general direction and then "feel around" for the final area?

Evaluation *

The following are to be evaluated:

1. Awareness of the existence of the body parts and their names.
2. Awareness of the precise location of each part. This instrument is subjective in nature and will require judgment on the part of the test administrator. If the child clearly satisfies

---

* *Note:* Combined with the major factor of *body-image* in this evaluation are such variables as laterality, directionality, control and rhythm.

Measurement of Perceptual-Motor Functioning 85

both items listed under evaluation, then he could be considered to have established a body-image. If there is hesitancy in identification or precise location of several of the body parts, then the child could benefit from additional work on body-image. If there is failure on a large number of items, the indication would be definite lack of body-image.

Considerations for Assessment

Considerations are listed below.

1. Give clear, distinct verbal commands.
2. Try to express the command as something that is "fun."
3. A slight hesitancy with the command "touch your elbows" is permitted, since many children are startled at the change in posture required.

LATERALITY

Closely associated with building a body-image and with possessing an awareness of our bodies is the normal process of learning the distinction between the right and left sides of our bodies. The external world through which we move does not have a blueprint with objective directions for locating objects which surround us. External objects are situated to the right, left, up, down, near or far only in relation to our own bodies. If a child has not developed the internal concept of left and right, his perceptual efficiency in coping with the external environment will be impaired.

Test for Laterality

The following simple test can be used to determine if a child has formed a concept of the right and left sides of his own body.

Materials Needed

Mats, rugs, blankets or towels are used.

Procedure

Ask the individual to stand facing you at a distance where he will be easily visible. Place the mat, or similar material, by his side for the items which require a prone position. Explain that you are going to give him a series of verbal commands, and that after each command, he is to do what was asked.

Verbal Commands (Eyes Closed)

1. Put or raise your right arm out away from your body (any position).
2. Pick up or move your left leg (any height).
3. Put or raise your left arm out away from your body (any position).
4. Pick up or move your right leg (any height).
5. Turn your head to the right.
6. Turn your head to the left.
7. Roll onto your left side (from either a back or stomach position on the mat).
8. Roll onto your right side (from a position on the mat.)

Test for Laterality and Midline

Procedure

Using the same materials and procedure as described above, the following additional commands should be given to determine if the laterality concept is present when the child is required to cross the midline of his body.

Verbal Commands

All items should be done first with the eyes open, then repeated with the eyes closed.

1. Put your right hand on your left shoulder.
2. Put your left hand on your right leg.
3. Put your left hand on your right shoulder.
4. Put your right hand on your left leg.
5. Touch your left hand to your right foot.

6. Touch your right knee with your left hand.
7. Touch your right hand to your left foot.
8. Touch your left knee with your right hand.
9. Cross your left leg over your right leg (from a prone position).
10. Touch the floor on the right side with your left hand (prone position).
11. Cross your right leg over your left leg (prone position).
12. Touch the floor on the left side with your right hand (prone position).

Evaluation

Either a pass or fail is given for each of the test items. If there is a hesitancy in any response, this should be scored as a fail.

Considerations for Assessment

These are as follow:

1. Verbal commands should be clear, distinct and given slowly.
2. Allow the individual to open his eyes between items to avoid dizziness.

DIRECTIONALITY

If an individual has successfully completed the stages of building a body-image and establishing an internal awareness of the distinction between his right and left sides, he is then ready to transfer these concepts of direction to his external world of space. During the developmental period, young children can be observed constantly exploring different movement patterns which are initiated toward various objects situated in the external space of their environment. With a firm concept of laterality established, they soon learn that these objects for which they are reaching are located to their right, their left, up above them or down below them.

Although we have separated the foundational elements of body-image, laterality and directionality, the problem involving spatial orientation is sometimes not quite so simple. With many of the children who have learning problems, it will be possible to identify a lack of development in one or more of these specific areas. For others, it may not be as easy to pinpoint the specific area. The important thing we want to emphasize is that if a child exhibits any difficulty in relating to his spatial world, he should be provided with developmental experiences in these areas. Lashley[42] reminds us of this importance by pointing out that every stimulus has a space setting and that the memory trace of external stimuli is associated with the space coordinates of our postural system.

Beter-Cragin Test of Oral Directions-Motor Responses

This test is suggested for use in determining directionality.

Materials Needed

Checklist of test items, a ball, a mat, several colored lines.

Procedure

Explain to the individual that you are going to give him a series of commands and that he is to listen carefully to each command and respond by doing what is asked.

Verbal Commands

1. Put an object *under* the table.
2. Put an object on *top* of the box.
3. Go and kneel on the *left side* of the mat.
4. Go and lie on the mat on your *stomach*.
5. Get a ball and throw it *up*.
6. Get a ball and throw it *down*.
7. Go and lie on the mat on your *back*.
8. Walk on the *(color)* line as *slowly* as possible.
9. Walk on the *(color)* line as *fast* as possible.

Measurement of Perceptual-Motor Functioning 89

10. Jump *up* and land as *quietly* as you can on two feet.
11. Jump *up* and land with two feet making a lot of *noise*.
12. Make your body as *small* as possible
13. Make your body as *long* as possible.
14. Walk on the *(color)* line, turn *right* and come back.
15. Walk on the *(color)* line, turn *left* and come back.
16. Walk *frontwards* or *forward* with your eyes closed.
17. Walk *backwards* with your eyes closed.
18. Walk *around* and make a circle.
19. Bend and touch the floor in *front* of you.
20. Bend and touch the floor in *back* of you.

Evaluation

The individual is given either a pass or fail for each of the test items.

Considerations for Assessment

These are listed below.

1. This test should be administered to one person at a time.
2. The verbal commands should be given clearly and slowly; if the tester feels that the individual has not understood the directions, the command may be repeated.

Beter-Cragin Bean Bag Test for Directionality

This test is very useful for determining whether a child has transferred directional concepts to external space.

Materials Needed

Needed are four small bean bags and four wooden frames (2' × 2').

Procedure

The frames are placed on the floor as shown in Figure 13. The individual stands outside of one of the frames, facing inward toward the frames.

90   *The Mentally Retarded Child and His Motor Behavior*

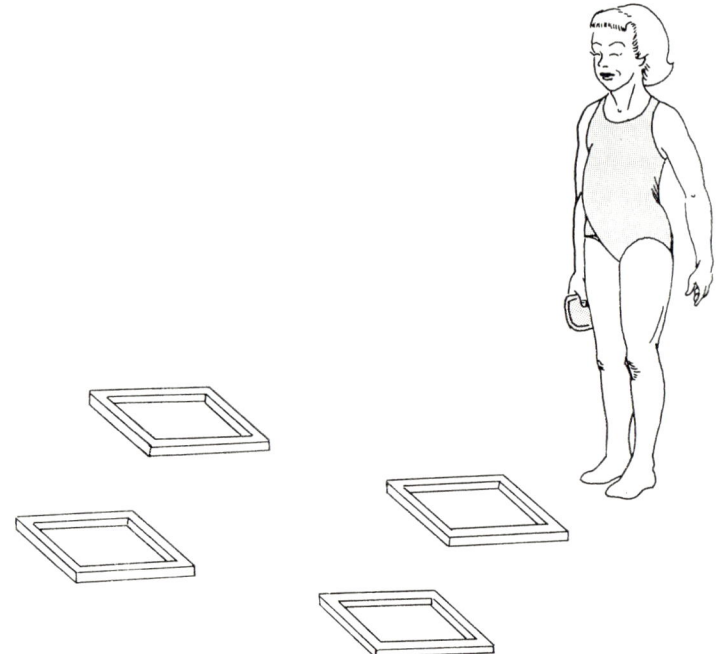

Figure 13. Beter-Cragin Bean Bag Test.

Verbal Commands

The individual should use his dominant hand.

1. Throw a bean bag to the frame on your *right*.
2. Throw a bean bag to the *top* frame (the one farthest from you).
3. Throw a bean bag to the *left* frame—the one on your left.
4. Throw a bean bag to the *bottom* frame (the one closest to you).

The person being tested should then be moved to a position in front of a different frame and the verbal commands are repeated. This procedure is continued until he has done the commands from a position in front of each of the four frames.

Modified Bean Bag Test

The previous test can be modified by having the individual stand in the center with the frames surrounding him as shown

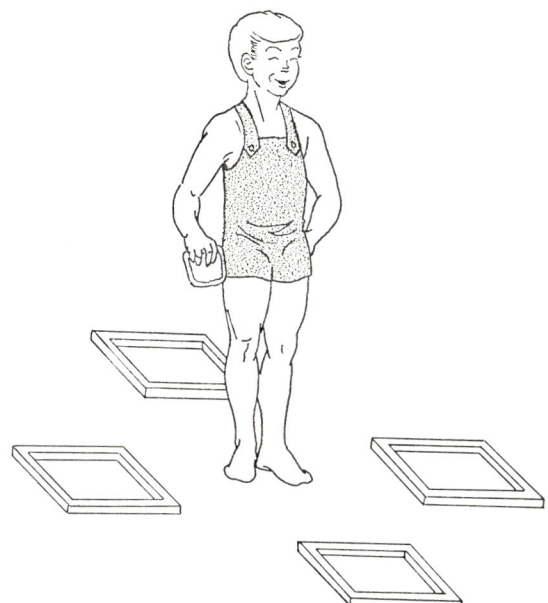

Figure 14. Modified Bean Bag Test.

in Figure 14. The commands in this case would be, "Throw the bean bag to the frame on your *right*, on your *left*, to the frame in *front* of you, and the frame *behind* or *in back* of you."

Scoring

The scoring for both tests would be simply pass or fail on each of the commands given. It should be pointed out, however, that total evaluation of directionality would depend upon performance of a complete rotation of body positions. Many times an individual will correctly identify the frames from the initial position, but when his position is changed, will be unable to make the proper directional transfer.

Considerations for Assessment

Below are some considerations for assessment.

1. These tests should be administered to one person at a time.
2. The verbal commands should be given clearly and slowly.

TEMPORAL RELATIONSHIPS

Another important aspect of behavior and of foundational development involves the organization of sensory data into synchronized units in time. Although this area has been the subject of discussion in professional literature, it could very likely be the least well-understood aspect of human behavior.

Kephart[39] discusses it as temporal dimension and suggests that it involves three aspects: (1) synchrony, (2) rhythm, and (3) sequence. It is probably not too important how you define temporal relationships, as long as the concept is recognized as being important to the learning process. The authors have chosen to use only the word *rhythm* to describe this phase of developmental orientation.

According to Mead,[48] rhythmic experiences may be categorized according to the manner in which they are perceived. *Auditory* rhythmic structures are organizations of time events, namely sounds. *Visual* rhythmic structures are organizations of space events, objects, animals or materials that can be seen. A third type of rhythmic experience would be *proprioceptive*. Body movement becomes a rhythmic experience because it involves a space-time organization of events. Any body movement involves the displacement of a body segment, and this movement or displacement is from one point to another through space and consumes a certain amount of time.

The extent to which rhythm is involved in human behavior has not been clearly pinpointed as yet. The fact that it plays a significant role, however, is becoming increasingly recognized. There has been a great deal of interest recently in investigating the aspect of rhythm. It is generally believed that there could be a significance in the rhythmic effects of such things as the constant rhythmic sounds of the mother's breathing and heartbeat inside the womb and the rocking of small babies. The authors have found an empirical relationship between lack of rhythmic organization and learning difficulties in children with whom they have been working. It seems, then, that almost from the moment of conception throughout life we are continually involved with the rhythmic organization of both internal and external stimuli. To the extent that man moves rhythmically, to the extent that he has perceptual sensitivity to all rhythm, to that extent does he experience the aesthetic joy of a harmonious relationship between his internal and external environments.[48]

Since there has not been enough research done to ferret out the exact nature and function of rhythmic organization in human behavior, there has also been a lack of adequate tests developed for measuring the ability. Undoubtedly, auditory, visual and proprioceptive organization of stimuli are involved in some of the behavioral components already discussed. We feel that many items on the Beter-Cragin Oral Commands Test will reflect poor temporal relationships, and that this instrument could be used in evaluating this aspect of behavior. Tests which have been developed to measure rhythm so far deal entirely with either music or dance. Although it is basically a test of dance ability, there are two subtests of the Harvey Rhythm Test which we feel can be effectively used to identify poor rhythmic organization.[32]

Rhythmic Dexterity of the Hands

This test measures the ability to organize auditory, visual and proprioceptive stimuli and make the appropriate motor response.

Materials Needed

Two wooden frames (fifteen inches square), eight wooden blocks (one and one-half inches square), a tape recorder and tape with instructions and meter for the test recorded on it are needed. (The directions for the Harvey Rhythm Test suggest that the test instructions and meter be recorded on tape, so that uniformity can be maintained. The authors have been using a tape in the testing they have done with mentally retarded children, but we feel that verbal instructions by the test administrator would serve as well and in some cases would be preferable. The exact instructions and the suggested meter are given below and the reader may choose to record them or not. Although any instrument could be used to beat out the given meter, it is suggested that a metronome be used to insure consistency.)

Instructions

Assume a kneeling position in front of the frames placed on the floor. Frame 1 contains eight blocks and is located on one side of you. Frame 2 is empty and is located on the other side of you. Move the blocks one by one from Frame 1 with one hand until all eight blocks are in Frame 2. Then, with the same hand, remove the blocks in the same manner back to Frame 1. Your movements are to be in rhythm with the given meter. It takes two beats to move one block from one frame to the other. The rhythm will be thirty-two beats—meter of eighty.

pick-up put-in pick-up put-in pick-up put-in pick-up put-in
| 1 | 2 | 3 | 4 | 5 | 6 | 7 | 8 |
| 9 | 10 | 11 | 12 | 13 | 14 | 15 | 16 |

Repeat.

Procedure

Several practice trials should be given before starting the test. During the practice trials, the verbal commands of "pick-up, put-in" should accompany the metronome beat. When the actual test is administered, however, only the metronome beat is heard and the movements of the hands must be in rhythm with the given meter.

Scoring

The following rating scale is used to score the test:

Measurement of Perceptual-Motor Functioning

Score

A. Each movement begins and ends in rhythm throughout the exercise. 4

B. Movements during the first two or the last two beats are out of rhythm with the given beat. Eight or seven blocks (according to the adjustment made to get in rhythm) are returned to the first frame. The remaining thirty beats are executed in rhythm. 3

C. Movements during the first sixteen beats are out of rhythm with the given beat. Eight or seven blocks (according to the adjustment made to get in rhythm) are returned to the first frame. The remaining sixteen beats are executed in rhythm. 2

D. Movements are jerky and in rhythm spasmodically throughout the given beat of the exercise. Eight or seven blocks (according to the adjustment made to get in rhythm) are returned to the first frame. 1

E. Each movement begins and ends out of rhythm throughout the given beat of the exercise. 0

Considerations for Assessment

Some considerations are listed below.

1. The test may be administered with the frames and blocks placed on a table and the individual seated instead of in the kneeling position.

TABLE XIII
PERCENTILE RANK NORMS FOR RHYTHMIC
DEXTERITY OF THE HANDS

Boys		Girls	
Percentile Rank	Raw Score	Percentile Rank	Raw Score
100	4	100	4
67	3	75	3
59	2	64	2
48	1	57	1
42	0	53	0

Based on the scores of 53 boys and 44 girls (classified as Educable Mentally Retarded) in the Dallas-Hurst-Denton, Texas area.

96   *The Mentally Retarded Child and His Motor Behavior*

2. Demonstration, explanation and practice are very important before actually administering the test. It will be necessary to make sure the person understands that he will only hear the click of the metronome and that he must keep time with the beat.

Varied Movement and Rhythms Performed in Wooden Frames Placed on the Floor

This test measures the ability to organize auditory, visual and proprioceptive stimuli and make the appropriate gross motor response.

Materials Needed

Four wooden frames (fifteen inches square), a tape recorder and tape and a metronome are needed. The tape is optional as previously explained.

Procedure

Place the four wooden frames on the floor as shown in Figure 15. Have the person take a position standing outside of Frame 1, facing Frame 4.

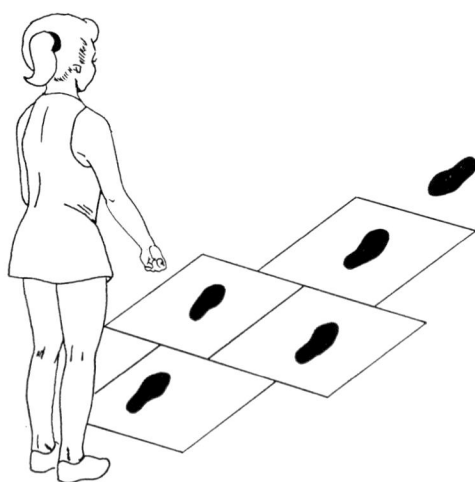

Figure 15. Varied movement and rhythms performed in wooden frames.

Instructions

Step into Frame 1, on the count of one, with one foot. Count two, jump landing on both feet, with one foot in Frame 2 and one foot in Frame 3. Count three, step in Frame 4 with one foot. Count four, step out of Frame 4 and turn around ready to repeat the same movement series back to the starting position. One, two, three, four; step, jump, step, turn. The movement will resemble the game of hopscotch. Every first beat of the four-beat series will be accented. Continue the steps and jumps until the beat stops. The rhythm will be four series of four beats—meter of 104.

step jump step turn step jump step turn step jump step turn
  1   2   3   4   1   2   3   4   1   2   3   4
repeat

Allow several practice trials of just the movements through the frames, and then use verbal commands of "step, jump" with the metronome beat. When the individual is ready, administer the test with only the beat of the metronome.

Scoring

Use the following rating scale to score the test:

	Score
A. The steps and jumps are executed in rhythm throughout the given beat of the exercise.	4
B. The steps and jumps are executed out of rhythm during the first four beats. The remaining series of four beats are executed in rhythm.	3
C. The steps and jumps are executed out of rhythm during the first two series of four beats. The remaining two series of four beats are executed in rhythm.	2
D. The steps and jumps are executed in a different movement pattern from the established movement pattern. However, the steps and jumps are executed in rhythm with the given beat throughout the exercise.	1
E. The steps and jumps are executed out of rhythm throughout the given beat of the exercise.	0

TABLE XIV

PERCENTILE RANK NORMS FOR VARIED MOVEMENT
AND RHYTHMS PERFORMED IN WOODEN FRAMES

Boys		Girls	
Percentile Rank	Raw Score	Percentile Rank	Raw Score
100	4	100	4
84	3	87	3
68	2	80	2
55	1	71	1
44	0	48	0

Based on the scores of 53 boys and 44 girls (classified as Educable Mentally Retarded) in the Dallas-Hurst-Denton, Texas area.

Considerations for Assessment

Listed below are some considerations.

1. Demonstration, explanation and practice are very important before actually administering the test. It will be necessary to make sure the person understands that he will only hear the click of the metronome and must keep time with the beat.

2. An assistant should be used to straighten the frames if they are kicked out of place during the test.

SENSORY EFFICIENCY

The efficiency with which an individual uses his sensory modalities is an inherent part of perceptual-motor functioning and as such, is inextricably involved in the previously discussed aspects of evaluation. There are many methods by which sensory efficiency can be evaluated, but to cover the information completely is beyond the scope of this chapter or this book. We would only like to present some very simple examples of tests which will help to identify weaknesses in specific sensory modalities.

Auditory Efficiency Test

This test measures auditory attention span and discrimination.

Materials Needed

Inflated balls of various sizes and a blindfold are used.

Procedure
Place the individual in a standing position in a fairly large-sized area and ask him to close his eyes, or place a blindfold over the eyes. The tester then bounces balls of various sizes in front of, in back of, to the right, and to the left of the individual. The person being tested is required to identify the position of the tester from the sound of the ball bouncing. He may make the identification with a verbal response of "to the right, left," and so forth, or by a motor response of pointing to the front, back, and so forth. The tester should start by using larger balls and bouncing the ball hard several times in each position; then, he should progress to smaller balls, lighter bounces and fewer times.

Scoring
A subjective evaluation must be made by the tester as to the efficiency with which the individual is able to respond to auditory stimuli. The person being tested will either be able to identify the position of the bounce or not, but observations should be made of the quickness with which the response is made and the differences in responses when the size of the ball and the intensity of the bounce are changed.

Considerations for Assessment
The person bouncing the ball should move quietly from one position to another so that the individual being tested cannot sense the position.

Visual Efficiency Test
Measures visual attention span and discrimination.

Materials Needed
Fifteen or twenty balls of different sizes and colors and a container for holding the balls are required.

Procedure
Two people are needed to administer the test, one to throw the balls and one to catch them. They are seated on the floor

about ten feet apart, and the individual to be tested is seated midway between the two testers. The test consists of the following three parts:

1. Colors: One test administrator selects balls of the same size but different colors without the testee being able to see them. He should start with two balls, then three, four, five, and so on. He throws the balls quickly to the other tester who catches them and places them in a container behind his back. The testee is then asked to identify the color of the first ball, the second, etc.

2. Size: One test administrator selects balls of the same color but different sizes and proceeds as described above.

3. Color and size: The third part of the test involves varying both the size and color of the balls thrown, but the procedure is the same as in Parts 1 and 2.

Scoring

A check for correct response and zero for incorrect can be used to score each item of the test. If a majority of items are missed, particularly when three or more balls are used, the individual probably has a weakness in this area.

Considerations for Assessment

Throw all balls as straight as possible in a horizontal plane.

Tactile Efficiency Test

Tactile discrimination is measured in this test.

Materials Needed

About fifteen objects of different shapes, sizes and surfaces and a large container are needed.

Procedure

All objects are placed in the container. The individual to be tested is blindfolded and asked to reach into the container and choose one object at a time. As he picks each object out of the container, he is asked to describe its shape, size and surface.

Scoring

The individual is given one point for correctly identifying each characteristic of the items in the container. If a majority of items are incorrectly identified, there is probably a weakness in this area.

Along with these simple tests of auditory, visual and tactile efficiency, the results of tests of kinesthetic perception given in Chapter 5 should be used for a total evaluation of sensory efficiency.

Chapter 7

MOVEMENT EXPERIENCES DESIGNED TO DEVELOP FACTORS OF PHYSIOLOGICAL EFFICIENCY AND COMPLEX MOTOR PERFORMANCE

> An abstraction given head,
> A giant on the horizon, given arms,
> A massive body and long legs stretched out
> Imposing forms they can not describe,
> Requiring order beyond their speech.
>
> —METHENY

ALL MOVEMENT, as previously emphasized by the authors, should be *meaningful* and *purposeful* in design, but the experience to the mover should be one of joyful play. As the child masters a movement, the more skillful he becomes and the more fun it is for him to *play* with this movement. Spontaneously, then, the child unfolds and begins to invent his own variations. He may run while bouncing a ball, he may walk or run forward and backward, or jump. Every new activity demands a different adjustment. Thus movement becomes perfected; coordinations refined; running becomes faster; jumping lighter and springier, higher and farther; climbing more dexterous; and catching more sure. Through a growing *confidence* in movement, there emerges an *awareness* of the body as a wholly integrated being.[22]

In order to insure that a growing confidence does occur, the following three steps should serve as guidelines in the planning of all movement experiences:

1. Discover the movement readiness characteristics of the youth's stage of development.

2. Prepare the environment so that the individual can exercise this readiness at will and without undue hazard.

3. Challenge the youth with additional related tasks designed to provide maximal diversification and to insure development of readiness.[22]

COMPONENTS OF PHYSIOLOGICAL EFFICIENCY

In order to be successful, movement experiences designed to develop muscular strength and endurance, cardiovascular endurance and flexibility must be planned with the following basic principles as a guide:

1. Desire: Some provision must be made to extract and maintain a desire on the part of the performer to want to develop physiological efficiency.

2. Systematic: The program should be implemented according to the *individual* goals or needs of each performer and should progress in difficulty and intensity.

3. Overload: Each activity should involve a workload which is slightly greater than the individual is capable of doing.

4. Regular: The activities should be engaged in on a regular basis at least twice a week and preferably three times a week.

5. Vigorous: Each program of activities should include some vigorous movement with large muscle involvement. (This will be determined by the physical capacity of each performer.)

6. Tapering off: Each session of activities should end with a tapering off involving enjoyable movement activities.

7. Relaxation: The program should be followed by a period of relaxation.

Muscular Strength

Arms and Shoulders

The following developmental experiences can be done in a standing, sitting or lying position. Vary the position and the size of the balls.

1. Using any size ball (as large as or larger than a volley-

ball), have the individual press on either side of the ball as hard as possible.

2. Using a rope, cord, rubber hose or inner tube (about one foot long), have the individual pull on the rope as hard as possible.

3. Have the individual hang from a horizontal bar with the body fully extended and feet off the floor. When the individual is able to do this without difficulty, have him hang with the arms in a flexed position.

4. Weight lifting: Using sandbags, bricks or commercial weights of various pounds, have the individual lift the weights with both a flexing and extending movement of the arms. Gradually increase the poundage of the weights.

Below are some further considerations.

1. As much as possible, make the above activities a problem-solving experience by asking such questions as, "How hard can you press on the ball?" "How hard can you pull on the rope?" "How long can you hang on the bar?"

2. Let the individual create his own movements from the above experiences.

3. Assist in counting the time of each experience. For example, pressing the ball, count one, two, three, etc. Gradually increase the count.

4. Check the arms to make sure each arm is pressing, pushing or pulling with equal force.

Abdomen

Listed below are some movement experiences.

1. Curl down: From a sitting position on the mat, knees bent and arms folded, start a backward movement toward the mat. Stop when you are about halfway down and hold the position for a count of four. Gradually increase the count.

2. Leg curl: Lie on the back and curl the legs slowly into the chest. Bend at the knees as the lift of the legs begins. As the legs are lowered, begin straightening them *slowly*.

Make sure the lower back maintains contact with the mat throughout the movement.

3. Sit-up: Start in a back-lying position on the mat with the hands behind the neck, legs bent and a partner holding the feet. Move forward to a sitting position. Stop about halfway up and hold the position for a count of four. Gradually increase the count.

Below are some additional ideas.

1. Use problem-solving questions such as "How long can you stay in this position?" "How slowly can you straighten your legs?" Also, assist by counting for the holding positions.

2. Use partners for motivation, sociability and perhaps for learning the movement sooner.

3. Let the individuals create their own movements.

Legs

Movement experiences for the legs follow below.

1. Use a rope, rubber hose or other appropriate material. Have the individual lie on his back on the mat. Bend one leg and place the rope under the feet. Grasping the end of the rope with both hands, try to extend the leg while pulling as hard as possible on the rope. Alternate legs. This can also be done in a standing position.

2. Broad jump: In a standing position, knees bent and arms behind the body, have the individual jump forward as the arms are swung forward and land on both feet.

3. Duck walk: Have the individual squat down as far as possible, extend the arms to either side and walk forward, backward and sideways.

Ask the following questions as each activity is performed: "How far can you extend your leg?" "How long can you hold it in that position?" "How far can you jump in one jump, two jumps, three jumps?" (measure the distance) "How far can you walk very slowly, quickly, before falling?"

Muscular Endurance

Since muscular endurance involves continuous exertion of a muscle or group of muscles, the important element in developmental activities is *repetition*. Three of the tests for muscular endurance given in Chapter 4 can also be used as activities for developing endurance. With these and the other activities listed below, the number of repetitions should be gradually increased as the individual gains in endurance.

Legs

The Squat Jumps described in Chapter 4, can be used to develop muscular endurance of the legs.

Abdomen

Sit-ups, as described in Chapter 4, can be used for developing abdominal endurance.

Arms and Shoulders

Some examples are given below.

1. Chin-ups or pull-ups: These are described for boys in Chapter 4. Girls should do the bar hang described under "Muscular Strength" in this chapter.
2. Push-ups.
    a. Boys: From a straight-arm front-leaning position, the individual lowers the body until the chest touches the mat; then he pushes upward to a straight-arm support. A straight body line should be maintained throughout.
    b. Girls: The same procedure as described above is followed, except that it is done from the knees instead of the toes.
3. Crab walk: With the hands and feet on the floor, head facing upward, walk backward, forward and sideward. Try to keep the hips up and the trunk as parallel to the floor as possible.

Further Considerations

Ask the problem-solving questions as previously suggested.

Flexibility

Johnson and Nelson[37] noted that a loss in flexibility is frequently regarded as one of the first signs that an individual is getting "out of shape." Generally speaking, a loss in flexibility will usually be an indication that a person is becoming less physically active. This principle will hold true for most retarded children, because they are usually more inactive than average children. The authors have noted, however, that mongoloid children are unusually flexible despite inactivity. This is undoubtedly due to their peculiar chemical makeup and should not be regarded as an indication that they are totally fit in all areas.

Lower Back and Leg Stretch

Examples are as follow.

1. From a standing position, bend at the waist and slowly bob to increase the downward movement of the trunk until you can touch the floor without bending the knees.

2. Sit on the mat with the legs spread apart and the back erect. Slowly bob forward and touch the floor between the legs, trying to increase the distance with each of ten bobs. Repeat the movement to the right leg and then to the left leg.

Shoulder Extension

The individual should take a lying position on the stomach with the arms straight above the head and about shoulder-width apart. A towel, rag or stick is grasped at either end and raised upward while keeping the chin on the floor and the elbows and wrists straight.

Trunk Extension

The individual lies on the mat on the stomach and a partner holds his feet and hips down. With the hands placed behind the neck, the individual then raises the trunk as far backward as possible.

Muscle Shortening

Movements for muscle shortening which were described in Chapter 3 can also be used.

Further Considerations

Listed below are some additional suggestions.
1. Ask problem-solving questions as previously suggested.
2. Move very slowly in the various positions, gradually increasing the angles at the joints involved.

Cardiovascular Endurance

Cardiovascular endurance is developed by engaging in activities which involve a vigorous workload. Care must be taken, however, to insure that undue fatigue does not result when unfit individuals are first beginning the movement program. There should be a gradual building of the amount of time of the performance so that endurance can be developed proportionately.

Movement Experiences

Several ideas follow below.

1. All movements mentioned under muscular strength and muscular endurance, if performed without a rest and in a relatively short period of time, will enhance cardiovascular endurance.
2. Run in place: Standing in a stationary position, the individual lifts his legs alternately, bringing the knees up higher and higher each time. To start, have him run in place for about five seconds and then walk around. Gradually increase the amount of time and height of the leg lift.
3. Rope skipping (straight or rebound skipping): Many variations and a great deal of creativity can be included in this activity. Depending upon the skill of the individual, use either counts or periods of time for endurance development.
4. Walk very fast (do not run), moving the arms up high, around a relatively large area.
5. Hop on one foot about ten feet away and hop back on the other foot.

6. Jump up and down on a rubber tire (timed or counts).

7. Walk to a designated area, run a short distance, then jump three times.

8. Crab walk to a designated distance, roll over to a prone position; then, with the arms folded across the chest, duck walk back.

9. Various relays with a small number of people and a short distance apart.

It is well to keep the following in mind also:

1. The principle of gradually increasing the time or counts should be used with all of the above suggested activities. As the skill and endurance of the individual increases, the workload should be increased.

2. Problem-solving questions can also be effectively used with these activities.

The authors also recommend Cooper's[18] walk/run twelve-minute test as a daily exercise program of movement. It can also serve as a goal in itself for achieving the functional factors of everyday living.

Cooper Walk/Run Program

Plan and mark various distances covering two miles from start to finish. This can be done in a gymnasium, through the corridors of the school, or in an open area outside. The individual begins at the start of the course and continues to walk or run until twelve minutes have elapsed. At the end of twelve minutes, he notes the distance that he has covered. The distance covered is then checked according to the following chart:

Fitness Category	Distance Covered
Very poor	less than 1 mile
Poor	1 to 1.24 miles
Fair	1.25 to 1.49 miles
Good	1.50 to 1.74 miles
Excellent	1.75 miles or more

When planning the course, the distances necessary for using the chart should be noted. For purposes of motivating the children, however, any innovative way of marking the course is recommended. *Example:* Use the names of different kinds of stores, i.e. grocery, drug, bakery, and so forth.

Gradually induce the individual to continue walking or running for the twelve-minute period and keep records of the distance covered each time.

RELAXATION

All individuals need to relax, but since most of us do not do so naturally, we need to learn how to relax. This is particularly true of mentally retarded children. What is meant by relaxation, as it is being used in this section, is the kinesthetic awareness or feeling of tension and release from the muscular tension. Movement experiences for promoting relaxation in different parts of the body are given below.

Head and Neck [63]

Some movement experiences for head and neck follow.

1. Seated position on the floor or mat. The individual leans back on his hands and allows his head to drop forward loosely. The muscles at the back of the neck will be stretched by the weight of the head. Repeat the same movement backward, to the right and to the left.

2. Head swaying: Assume same position as described above. With a rolling movement, allow it to drop until the ear is directly over one shoulder; then allow the head to swing forward, downward and over the opposite side.

Shoulder Girdle [63]

Movements for the shoulder girdle are given below.

1. Seated position in a chair or standing. Keeping the trunk erect (check the spine), elevate or lift one shoulder at a time and allow it to *drop* back into place. Keep the arms dangling and hanging at the sides. Try one shoulder, then the other and then both. Ask the individual to reach with shoulder.

Check the dropping motion to make sure a release of tension is occurring.

2. Seated position in a chair. Keeping the trunk erect and arms dangling at the sides, the individual is instructed to pull the shoulder blades toward one another and then release them. Ask the individual to show you his wings. In the learning stages, you might lift the arms slightly to assist in contraction of the back muscles. Check between the shoulder blades for the correct movement. (Press lightly between the blades to help the person feel the motion.)

Arms [63]

Below are some examples of arm movements.

1. Lying position on the stomach or back on a mat or rug. Have the individual lift one arm about six inches off the mat, hold the position briefly and then quickly drop the arm. Repeat with the other arm.

2. Lying position on the back with the arms along the sides of the body. Instruct the individual to contract, squeeze or tighten the left arm, then relax or let go. Repeat for the right arm. Check to make sure sufficient tension is attained and that a complete release of tension occurs. In the beginning, some individuals may be able to achieve the contraction easier by squeezing the fist. They should be trained as soon as possible to consciously contract the muscles in the arm with the hand in the open position.

Trunk [63]

Standing in a side-stride position, drop the head forward and gradually slide the head down as the arms are sliding down each leg. Start back to an erect position by lifting the trunk first and the back of the head last.

Legs [63]

Lying position on the back with the legs slightly separated. Stretch or extend the left leg and then let it go as you would a rubberband. Repeat with the right leg and then with both legs at the same time. The individual should be trained to accomplish the above while keeping the rest of the body as relaxed as possible.

Further Considerations

As the skill develops, combine various areas of the body. For example, start by contracting the arms, then go to the shoulders while still contracting the arms, then add the trunk. Proceed with the relaxation in the same manner.

POSTURE

The human frame is not a very stable edifice. The trunk of the human body must balance and support the weights of the head, shoulders, and organs distributed at various positions along the spinal column, and it rests upon the legs and feet, which form a relatively small base of support. In addition to support of various body segments, our muscles are continuously at work to prevent us from collapsing against the constant pull of gravity. The constant struggle to keep the body erect against the pull of gravity puts more of a demand on some muscle groups than others and they are referred to as the *antigravity* muscles. Included in this group would be the following:

1. Between the shoulder blades and back of the neck (rhomboids and trapezius).
2. Abdominal wall (rectus abdominus).
3. Up the back to the head (spinal erectors).
4. Buttocks (gluteus maximus).
5. Front of the thigh (quadriceps).
6. Calf (gastrocnemius).
7. Sole of foot, inner border of foot and lower leg (numerous smaller muscles).[43]

As a result of inadequate daily exercise, prolonged stretching of a muscle group or a body segment being carried for too long in an off-balance position, our antigravity muscles tend to become weakened. For the majority of postural problems, then, exercises designed to strengthen the appropriate muscles will alleviate the problem. The following exercises represent examples of those which can be used for some of the different antigravity muscle groups.

Shoulder Blades and Back of the Neck

The following are suggested exercises:

1. Shoulder girdle alignment: Lie on the mat in a prone position, forehead resting on the mat and hands clasped behind the back. Adduct (pull together) the shoulder blades very tightly and then relax them. Repeat the exercise several times and gradually increase the number of repetitions.

2. Mid-shoulder strengthening: Lie on the mat on the stomach with the legs extended and arms along the sides. Have someone place a weight in each hand. Adduct the shoulder blades (pull together), raise the arms together as high as possible, keeping the chin on the mat and the shoulder blades squeezed together. Start with weights which can be lifted without undue strain and when they can be lifted more than ten times, increase the poundage.

3. Lower neck and upper back strengthening: Use a rope or piece of rubber tubing. Loop the rope twice in front of the chest. Grasp the rope with the palms toward the body and as close to the chest as possible. Keep the elbows even with the shoulders and pull out with your arms.

4. Neck strengthening: Fold a towel or similar piece of material lengthwise twice. Standing with the back straight, but shoulders relaxed, place the towel behind the head. Grasping one end in each hand, pull the towel forward with both hands. The forward movement of the head is then resisted by pressing the head backward. Repeat the exercise several times and gradually increase the number of repetitions.

Abdominal Wall

Abdominal wall exercises are described below.

1. Stretch exercises: Lie on the mat in a back-lying position

with the arms extended at the sides. Push your lower back (lumbar region) to the mat. It will help to keep the lower back flat on the mat if you contract the gluteal muscles (buttocks). With the lower back kept in contact with the mat, stretch your arms above the head and extend the legs and feet. Next stretch the arm and leg on one side of the body and relax the other side; then, alternate. Next stretch the left arm and right leg; then, right arm and left leg. *Make sure the lower back remains in contact with the mat throughout the exercise.*

2. Abdominal strenthening: Sit-ups, for developing abdominal strength, were described earlier in this chapter in the section on muscular strength and the reader is referred to that section.

Legs

Exercises for the legs follow.

1. Back of the legs: Lie on the mat on the back. Draw the right knee toward the chest, so that the thigh is perpendicular to the floor and the lower part of the leg is parallel to the floor. Using a piece of rope or a towel, place the rope around the bottom of the foot and grasp the ends with each hand. Push the leg as hard as possible against the rope, but prevent any movement of the thigh by holding the rope firmly. Hold this position for five or six seconds and relax. Repeat three times and then perform the exercise with the left leg.

2. Front of the legs: Sit on a table or other structure so that the legs hang over the edge. Hold the forward edge of the table with both hands and cross the feet so the left ankle is over the front of the right ankle. Push upward and forward as hard as possible with the right leg until it is straight, and at the same time offer resistance with the left leg so that the right leg can barely move. Return to the starting position by pushing downward and backward as hard as possible with the left leg while resisting with the right leg. Repeat five times with each leg.[9]

Feet

Below are some suggestions for exercising the feet.

1. Tightrope walker (done barefooted): Stand with one foot ahead of the other on a chalk (or other) line on the floor. While walking the line on tiptoe with exactness and care, turn the toes in and heels out and try to grasp the floor with the toes.[57]

2. Picking up marbles: Standing without shoes, pick up one marble with the toes and transfer it to the hand. Repeat several times.[57]

3. Walking with marbles: Place four marbles on the floor. Pick up two marbles with the toes of each foot and walk while holding the marbles with the toes.[57]

BALANCE

Balance is an important ability for many everyday living tasks and activities, such as walking, standing, stooping, pulling. Bass (7) pointed out that the ability to balance easily, whether statically or dynamically, depends upon the function of the mechanisms in the semicircular canals; the kinesthetic sensations in the muscles, tendons and joints; visual perception while the body is in motion; and the ability to coordinate these three sources of stimuli. Whelan,[78] in a later study, identified similar factors. They were general static-balance kinesthetic response, vertical semicircular canals, general ampullar-sensitivity and convergence of the eyes. Many research studies have examined the balance of retarded children as a group and have found out that these children do not balance as well as normal (typical) children. Hoffman[33] found that fast-learning groups tend to be superior to slow-learning groups on balance tests.

Kephart[39] noted that children must experiment until they feel and realize from their own movement (kinesthetic feedback) that their bodies are balanced by their right and left areas. A child must develop a right-left gradient with his movements in terms of his relationship to gravity. The awareness of right and left develops and stabilizes from the use of *balance and posture*. The child learns that when he leans too far to the right and does not right or correct himself by leaning to the left or by supporting himself better, he will fall over. Balance is very important in establishing *laterality* and should be included with laterality movements.

Low to moderate correlations have been obtained between balance and reading, as reported by Cratty[19] in a study conducted in the perceptual-motor learning laboratory at the University of California. Though more research is needed in the area of balance and the role it plays in the learning of mentally retarded children, present results seem to indicate that it is an important factor. Balance can be improved in a structured, purposeful, meaningful program of movement, as studies of Beter,[12] Cratty,[19] Espenschade,[27] Lafuze[41] and Smith[68] have reported.

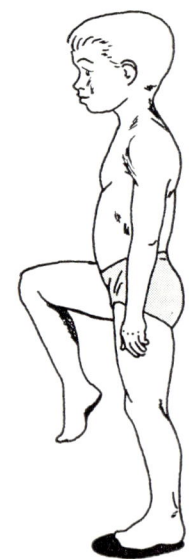

Figure 16. Foot balance.

Movement Factors of Physiological Efficiency 117

Static Balance

Suggested movement experiences which will aid in developing balance are presented below.

1. In a standing position, keep the left foot on the floor and flex the right leg as shown in Figure 16. The hands are placed on the hips and the person tries to maintain his balance as long as possible. Repeat with the right foot down and left leg up. For variation and progression, hold both arms above the head or out to the sides, or alternate the various arm positions while maintaining balance.

2. In a standing position, keep the left foot on the floor and bend the trunk forward. Extend the arms sideward and stretch the right leg backward as shown in Figure 17. Repeat with the right foot down and left leg back. Keep the supporting leg straight. Perform the movement first with the eyes open and then with the eyes closed and hold the position for various time periods.

Figure 17. Foot balance variation.

3. Stand on a designated line (two inches wide) with one foot in front of the other. Hold the arms above the head, out to the sides, folded on the shoulders and other modifications of increasing difficulty. Perform first with the eyes open and then with the eyes closed.

4. Take a kneeling position on the mat, as shown in Figure 18. Keep the left knee on the mat and raise the right leg up; then reverse knees. In the beginning, the arms may be in any position which will aid in maintaining balance. As the individual becomes more proficient, vary the position of the arms to increase difficulty. Perform first with the eyes open and then with them closed.

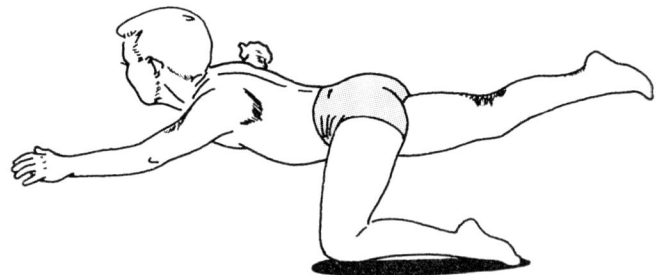

Figure 18. Knee balance.

Dynamic Balance

Line Walking

Ideas using lines are given below.

1. Using a line two inches wide, have the individual walk forward and backward with the eyes opened and closed. Vary the position of the arms as described under "Static Balance." Progress in difficulty by increasing the length of the lines and by creating courses with zig-zag patterns.

2. Mark two lines on the floor six inches apart and have the individual walk forward and backward with the eyes opened and closed; then, have the person walk forward, turn and come back. Vary the position of the arms and length of the lines for increasing difficulty.

Balance Beam

The balance beam can be used in the following ways:

1. Walk forward and backward with the eyes opened and closed.

2. Walk forward and backward while carrying an object (stick, golf club, ball or baton) with the eyes opened and closed.

3. Walk sidewards to the left, then right; then walk sidewards while carrying an object with the eyes opened and closed.

4. Place objects on the beam and walk over them.

5. Stoop and pick up an object with both feet on the beam, then keep one foot on the beam and raise the other leg up.

6. Catch, bounce or hit balls while walking the beam.

Nelson Balance Test [37]

The Nelson Balance Test, described in Chapter 5, can also be used as an activity for developing both static and dynamic balance.

Further Considerations

Below are some additional points to keep in mind.

1. Emphasize right and left movements with all of the suggested activities for laterality and directionality.

2. Time the various movements for motivation purposes.

3. Assist the individual to create his own movements by asking How and Why.

4. The difficulty of the static balance activities can be increased by decreasing the base of support or raising the center of gravity.

COMPLEX FACTORS OF MOTOR EFFICIENCY

As pointed out in Chapter 5, efficient movement for dealing with complex motor tasks involves such factors as speed of movement, reaction time, muscular power and agility. These are factors which contribute to skilled performance in such sports activities as basketball, volleyball, tennis and badminton. For most people, these specific factors develop as a result of engaging in a variety of physical activities from childhood through adulthood. The majority of mentally retarded children, however, have had limited opportunities for movement activities and they will be quite weak in most or all of these factors.

Before they can start to acquire complex sports skills, then, they will benefit from some basic activities requiring these specific abilities.

Reaction Time

Reaction time is considered as the elapsed time between the presentation of a stimulus and the initiation of a response. For a simple task requiring a response to an auditory or visual stimulus, the typical individual could be expected to concentrate and attend to the task. Their response time or reaction time, then, would represent more closely the amount of time for the messages to travel the neural pathways. When dealing with the reaction time of mentally retarded children, one has to consider also the elements of concentration and attention span. Many of the suggested activities which follow will be helpful in increasing concentration and attention span, as well as decreasing reaction time.

Reaction to a Visual Stimulus

MATERIALS NEEDED. Needed are red flags or colored pieces of cloth, bells with the button on top or small hand bells (if not available, any instrument which could be used to make a sound).

PROCEDURE. Have one or more individuals seated comfortably, but in an erect position. Place the bell or other instrument so that it is several inches from their dominant hand. Have a leader stand about five feet away from and in front of the group so that he can be clearly seen by all individuals. The leader will start with the flag behind his back and then quickly hold it out in view of the group. As soon as each individual sees the flag, he is to ring his bell. The leader should alternate the amount of time which elapses between a signal "ready" and the presentation of the flag (three seconds, five seconds, one second, etc.).

VARIATIONS. As soon as all individuals appear to completely understand the procedure and have reached the point of reacting quickly to the simple stimulus, the stimulus should be made increasingly more complex.

1. Use two flags of different colors. Instruct the group that they are to proceed as previously directed when the red flag appears, but do nothing if the other colored flag appears.
2. Use three flags of different colors. For the red flag, ring the bell once; the blue flag, twice; and the yellow flag do nothing.
3. Use two flags of different colors and give each individual a bell and a horn or whistle. If the red flag appears, they ring the bell; if the blue flag appears, they blow the horn or whistle.

Reaction to an Auditory Stimulus

The procedure outlined for reaction to a visual stimulus can just be reversed. This time the leader will use the bell and the group will be given the flags. The leader in this instance should have the bell hidden from the group so that they must depend entirely upon the sound as the stimulus. Each of the variations given in the previous section can be reversed in the same manner.

For motivation purposes, make some response to the results by identifying the winner each time.

Speed of Movement

Many mentally retarded children have difficulty with, or cannot tell time at all. As a result, they are unaware of the passage of time, and the concept of speed has not been developed. Typical activities such as the fifty-yard dash, the shuttle run and relays will have little significance until these concepts are developed. It is suggested, therefore, that activities to increase speed of movement remain simple in the beginning for those who lack the basic concepts. Any activity which the individual is already familiar with can be used, except that the time element is introduced. He is now required to do the familiar activity, but either in a specified period of time or with the amount of time is takes him to do it being recorded. For example, if the individual is working on balance, strength or ball bouncing, use a timer or stopwatch to call his attention to the amount of time which transpires from start to finish of the activity. Then compare the times from one performance to the next so that he begins to understand when he does something in a short period of time and when it takes him a long time.

Research has shown that speed of movement can be increased by increasing strength. A program of strength-developing exercises will, therefore, be beneficial along with specific activities designed to emphasize speed.

Speed of Movement and Reaction Time

The separation of these two factors in the previous sections was done because the authors felt that specific activities for each were appropriate for retarded children. When one is considering skilled performance of a complex motor task, it is really the combination of the two factors which produces the end result. For example, if two people are playing tennis and one reacts slowly but moves fast and the other reacts quickly but moves slowly, the end result in terms of hitting the ball across the net might well be the same. Activities which involve both factors should be provided for these individuals who are very weak in these areas.

Red Light

This game can be played with any number of players. A fairly large area, such as a gymnasium or playing field should be used. One person in the group is designated as "it" and he stands at one end of the field or gym. The other players line up behind a starting line at the other end. The player who is "it" counts out loud from one to ten and then shouts "Red light." When he starts counting, the other players try to advance as rapidly as possible toward the position of "it." When "it" says "Red light," he turns around quickly and identifies any player who is still in motion. Those players who are still moving must go back to the starting line. "It" then turns around and starts counting again and the game continues as before. The first person to reach "it" wins the game and he then becomes "it."

Further Considerations

Some additional points are listed below.

1. The teacher should make sure that all players identified as being in motion return all the way to the starting line.

2. The person who is "it" must count each number between one and ten and should say them distinctly.

Agility

Being able to rapidly change one's body position or the direction in which one is moving is also an ability which is necessary for performing complex motor tasks. As is true with many of the factors contributing to skilled motor performance, agility cannot be completely isolated from other factors such as balance and speed of movement. At one time it was believed that agility was dependent to a large extent upon heredity, but recent research has shown that it can be improved through practice and training. As has been pointed out in connection with other factors, a great many retarded children will not be able to change body position or to change the direction of their movement with skill. This lack of ability, however, can be changed through training and practice of activities which require this type of movement.

Dodge Run [28]

Set up four chairs, or other appropriate objects, in a line as shown in Figure 19. Have the person stand behind the starting line and on the signal "go" run as rapidly as possible in and out of the chairs in a figure-eight course. Record the amount of time it takes the person to cover the course from start to finish. Keep regular records for each person so that they can see the improvement they make.

Although they may do so in the beginning, the students

124 The Mentally Retarded Child and His Motor Behavior

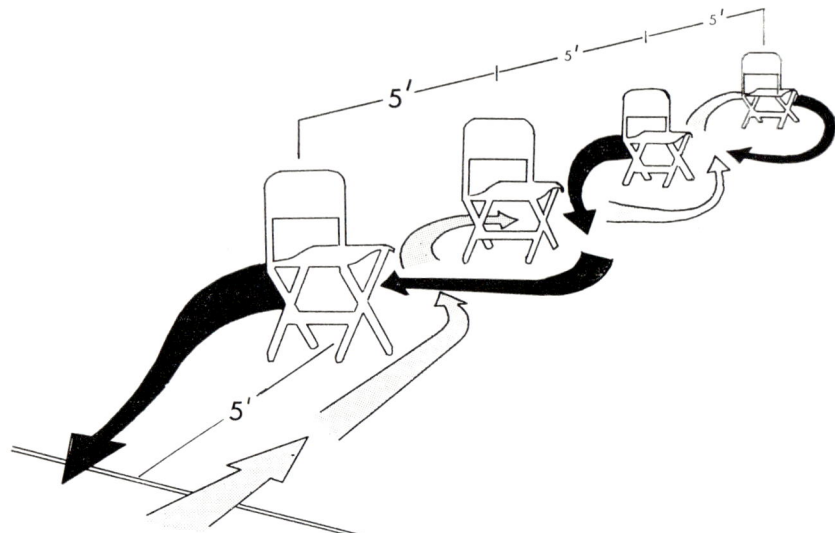

Figure 19. Dodge Run.

should be trained to move around the chairs without touching them. For individuals who are especially weak in agility, it is recommended that they be allowed to walk through the course in the beginning and gradually work up to the run.

Obstacle Run

Using an area approximately 15′ × 15′, set up an obstacle course which includes about five different obstacles requiring movement over, under, around, and so forth. Mark a starting line and a finish line. Have the individual begin from various positions (one time standing, then sitting, then lying) from behind the starting line, go through the obstacles and across the finish line as quickly as possible (see Figure 20).

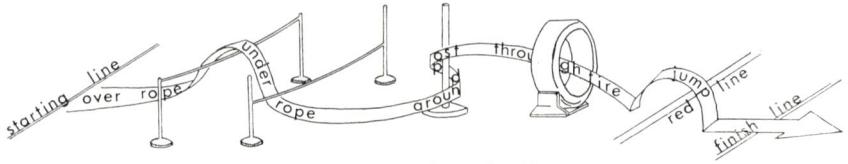

Figure 20. Obstacle Run.

It is suggested that you start with two or three obstacles and gradually increase the number. If some individuals are especially weak in agility, allow them to walk through the course in the beginning.

Quadrant Jump

The Quadrant Jump, described under agility testing in Chapter 5, can be used as an activity for developing agility.

Power

Athletic muscular power, required in many sports activities, depends to a large extent upon muscular strength and the skill involved in the specific task. It is the opinion of the authors that mentally retarded children who score low on tests of power will do so partly because of a lack of minimum strength and lack of skill. There are three tests of athletic power which can be effectively used to help improve power. The Standing Broad Jump and Medicine Ball Put were described in Chapter 5. These, along with the Vertical Jump, can be used as activities for the students to perform. All of these activities also offer an excellent opportunity to help teach the concepts of distance and units of measurement.

Vertical Jump [59]

MATERIALS NEEDED. A yardstick or tape measure, several pieces of chalk and a smooth wall surface which is at least twelve feet from the floor are needed.

DIRECTIONS. The individual should stand with one side toward the wall, heels together, and hold a one-inch piece of chalk in the hand nearest to the wall. Keeping the heels on the floor, he should reach up as high as possible and make a mark on the wall with the chalk. Continuing to hold the chalk in his fingers, the individual then should jump as high as possible and make another mark at the height of his jump. The distance is measured to the nearest half-inch between the reach mark and the jump mark.

Below are some ideas to keep in mind.

1. For the Standing Broad Jump and the Vertical Jump, time should be spent in instructing the students on the techniques involved in the two tasks. Bending the knees, timing the upward or outward movement with the extension of the legs and on the Broad Jump, using the arms to help propel the body forward should be practiced.

2. In all activities, continuous records of distances made by each person should be kept to help teach the concept of distance, as well as for motivation.

3. Allow the students to assist with the measurement so they can learn the units of measurement more readily.

The movement activities suggested in this chapter, for developing various factors of movement efficiency, are only a small sample of hundreds which are possible. The authors selected experiences which they felt were effective and which could be done with a minimum of special equipment. A further consideration was that the majority of these experiences could be used right in the classroom if a playing field or gymnasium is not available. Within any group of children who have been designated as retarded, there will be some who are at a low level of physical development and some who will be able to perform very well. The suggested activities are adaptable to all levels of skill.

CIRCUIT AND INTERVAL TRAINING

When the students have become familiar with and reasonably proficient at performing many of the exercises and movements suggested in this chapter, it might be beneficial to set up circuit or interval training for them.

Circuit Training

In the circuit-training movement program, the movements are considered as a unit composed of individual parts, between which there is no period of decreased activity. A number of selected movements are performed at areas arranged in a particular pattern, which permits a person to train or move at a load compatible with his individual capacity. There are two basic types of circuit programs commonly used.

1. Limited time circuit: The individual tries to complete three circuits of the course in a prescribed period of time (ten minutes is traditional).

2. Fixed circuit: The individual attempts to complete three circuits of the course and the time required to do so is recorded.

It is suggested that mentally retarded children start with the fixed circuit training and work up to the limited time circuit, trying for three complete circuits in the time limit.

Interval Training

In interval training, each part of the workout is timed or regulated individually, and a definite interval of decreased activity is planned between each exercise. During the recovery periods, the individual keeps moving with activities of a decreased intensity. Some of the variations used for the amount of movement performed during interval training include (1) speed or intensity of effort, (2) duration or distance of the effort, (3) number of times the effort is repeated, (4) length of the recovery period, and (5) the nature of the activity during the recovery period.

Chapter 8

MOVEMENT EXPERIENCES DESIGNED TO DEVELOP PERCEPTUAL-MOTOR EFFICIENCY

What we know in what we see,
What we feel in what we hear
What we are . . . and what we think

—METHENY

A *motor skill* is that act which is performed with a high degree of precision, and in which only limited variation is possible. A *motor pattern*, however, is a coordinated motor behavior composed of a combination of movements, adapted to serve a purpose. It is a motor generalization, allowing for a greater degree of variability. Motor patterns are essential for information gathering at a very *basic* stage of each child's development.[39] The early motor explorations of the child begin a long process of development, growth, and learning by which the child finds out about himself and the world around him. Motor experimentation and motor learning become the foundation upon which this knowledge is built, and the base upon which the entire personality of the child rests.[71]

By investigating the world through movement, a child learns to interpret these perceptual patterns in terms of information meaningful to him and in terms of information which can be used to influence his behavior in a way that more veridical and more efficient responses occur. Through exploratory movements, the child on one hand generates perceptual information and, on the other hand, relates this information to himself and his activities. A child builds a hierarchy of systematic knowledge based upon the foundation of his physical interaction with his environment. The importance of an adequate motor interaction, therefore, becomes apparent.[36] Glasscow[29] stated that performances of motor skills are dependent upon continuous feedback from the auditory, visual, muscular and joint senses, so perceptual processes are an integral part of any motor activity.

Movement *is* what movement *does*. By a carefully planned program of purposeful, sequential movement experiences. which progress from simple motor tasks to the more complex, the cognitive development of each individual can be further enhanced. This goal can be reached more effectively if certain supplementary aspects are incorporated into the movement experiences. The authors support Robinson's[58] thesis that retarded children make less use of verbal mediation in their silent thought processes, and that the employment of their words is poorly formulated and communicated in ideas. Individuals with learning difficulties need opportunities to explore and interact with their environment for perceptual growth, but they must also be helped to develop freedom from the dominance of environmental stimuli. This aspect of educating the child with a learning disability has received considerable attention by Luria, who has outlined what he feels is a definite process in reaching "voluntary behavior." According to Luria, the individual can be helped to reach voluntary behavior by being guided through the following stages, in this order:

1. Behavior is *controlled* by an adult's *verbal commands*.
2. Child directs his own behavior by verbalizing the commands.
3. Child controls his behavior silently by using thought processes or internal speech.[44,45]

It is strongly recommended by the authors, therefore, that the above stages be incorporated into the presentation of movement experiences suggested in this chapter.

Two other important aspects of insuring the development of cognitive processes are *novelty* and *variety*. Novelty, in this sense, is being used to mean variations of the familiar. It should involve proceeding from what is known to what is unknown in appropriately short steps. The work of Piaget points to the conclusion that the child must be challenged if cognitive growth is to occur. For many mentally retarded children, the stimulation patterns of their lives have remained constant for so long that they are in a habitual state of apathy. The *slightly novel task* will alert and attract the attention and motivate the performance of the individual. The second element important to cognitive growth involves variety of stimulation. Early theorists in education for perceptually handicapped children favored an educational environment in which stimulation was reduced to a minimum to prevent distraction. Recent research, however, tends to suggest that a variety of stimuli might be more beneficial to cognitive development. This is still an area which needs further investigation and in which practical applications need to be developed. Care must be taken to recognize and provide for the special needs of both the hypo- and hyperactive child, but an attempt should be made to aid these individuals in developing their inhibitory processes. This can be accomplished to some extent by using sharp, quick, novel and differing degrees of auditory stimulation for commands given during the suggested movement experiences in the following sections.

LOCOMOTOR MOVEMENT PATTERNS AND BASIC MOTOR SKILLS

Many of the movement experiences suggested in the latter part of this chapter require a minimum degree of ability in both locomotor movements and basic motor skills. It is recommended, therefore, that these abilities be developed first.

Locomotor Movement Patterns

The primary way in which the body moves is by pushing against a resistive force. Although there are many forms of locomotion, man generally moves by the action of the lower extremities in walking, running, leaping, jumping and hopping.

These locomotor movements then become the basic foundation of all future movements. Combinations of these basic movements are skipping, galloping and sliding. The following are selected experiences to develop locomotor abilities.

Walking

Several walking movements are described below.

1. Walk heel-toe forward and backward, swinging the arms vigorously.
2. Same as above, except walk on the balls of the feet and swing the arms vigorously in a circle formation.
3. Same as 1, but keep the arms above the head.
4. Walk fast and slowly in all of the above described ways.

Running

Runing exercises follow below.

1. This is a modification of walking in which the arms move at a more rapid rate, are flexed at the elbows and brought in close to the body.
2. Run and make a complete stop in various directions. Start with the feet in a forward stride position (one foot in front of the other with the trunk of the body inclined forward), push from both feet, run and stop on a signal with the knees flexed.
   a. Run forward and backward—stop on signal.
   b. Run forward, turn or circle right—stop on signal.
   c. Run forward, turn or circle left—stop on signal.
   d. Run forward and back to the starting position.
3. Run while controlling an object.
   a. Run a short distance while holding an object.
   b. Run a short distance while balancing an object on the head.
   c. Run, pick up an object and continue running.
   d. Run while bouncing a ball; then bounce the ball around obstacles.

4. Running variations.
   a. Walk—run.
   b. Run slowly, softly, quickly, with knees high and low.
   c. Run using a variety of movements and stop signals.

Leaping

Several leaping exercises can be used effectively.

1. Leaping for distance or height is an extension of running with a complete suspension into the air.
   a. For distance, leap across two ropes parallel to each other on the floor.
   b. For height, leap over a balance beam, rope or other obstacle; leap and touch or grab an object suspended overhead.
   c. Keep balloons suspended by leaping and tapping the balloon to keep it up in the air.
2. Combination of the leap and other locomotor movements.
   a. Leap, step, step, walk.
   b. Leap, step, step, run.
   c. Run, run, leap.
   d. Leap, walk, run, step.

Jumping

Jumping exercises are listed below.*

1. Vertical.
   a. Take off on one foot or both feet with or without a run.
   b. Jump, pressing the head toward an object placed vertically overhead, with or without a run.
   c. Jump, swinging the arms forward and backward, with or without a run.
   d. Jump, touching an object overhead with one or both hands, with and without a run.
   e. Jump over various objects, attaining height.

Note: In all jumping activities, make sure the knees are flexed upon landing.

2. Horizontal.
   a. Take off on one or both feet, with or without a run to increase the width of the jump.
   b. Do a standing long and broad jump.
   c. Hop, step and jump.
   d. Do a one-foot broad jump.
   e. Jump forward, backward and to alternate sides.
3. Variations in the air.
   a. Jump and turn.
   b. Jump from side to side over a rope.
   c. Jump and catch objects.
   d. Jump over marks on the floor and turn.

Hopping

The following list gives hopping exercises.

1. Hopping involves the transfer of weight from one foot to the *same* foot.
   a. Hop for either distance or height.
   b. Hop forward and backward; hop forward and return to starting position.
   c. Hop, changing feet, forward, backward, sideward and changing directions.
   d. Hop slowly, quickly; use large and small hops.
2. Variations.
   a. Hop with ropes, balls.
   b. Combine hops with runs, leaps, turns, jumps and steps.

Skipping, Galloping and Sliding

The skip, gallop and slide are all combinations of the preceding basic movements, performed in an uneven rhythmic pattern.

Gallop is a step with the leading foot and closing with the opposite foot. The foot that begins the step is always leading; the rear foot does not pass the leading foot on the close.

Slide is usually done in a sideward direction and consists of a step and close. The slide is performed more smoothly than the gallop.

Skip is a step and hop executed on the same foot and is a springy, joyful movement.

1. Skip in a straight line, in a circle, around objects and with ropes.
2. Gallop and slide in a straight line, around objects and in circles.
3. Combine all three movements in various directions and with various qualities of movement (e.g. slow, fast, quietly, with noise).

Basic Motor Skills

Styles of throwing vary widely depending upon the size of the ball used, the distance and speed desired, and the game in which the throw is being used. Large, colored balls and bean bags, thrown at short distances, are suggested in the beginning. Gradually increase the distance and decrease the size of the ball.

1. Underarm throw: The ball is grasped with the fingers of the dominant hand which is held in front of the body. At the same time, the throwing arm swings back, the trunk is inclined forward; the arm then swings forward and at the same time, a step is taken forward with the opposite foot.
    a. Throw at stationary targets on the wall, then at swinging targets such as a tire or dummy. (Numbers and letters can be used for targets.)
    b. Throw various-sized balls for distance. Ask "How far can you throw a ball?" "Which ball can you throw the farthest?"
    c. Throw balls into various-sized containers from a variety of directions and distances.
    d. Throw and catch with a partner.
2. Overarm throw: The ball is grasped with the fingers of the dominant hand and the opposite side is turned in the direction in which the throw is to be made. The weight is on the back foot and the trunk is inclined backward. The throwing arm is raised with elbow bent and about shoulder-high; then,

the arm is drawn back behind the shoulder. The throw is made by a quick reversal in all directions. The elbow starts forward and the hand is whipped past it. At the same time, the body is turned forward and the weight is thrown onto the forward foot. The arm is extended as the ball is released.

  a. The same activities used for the underarm throw are also suggested here, except smaller balls should be used in the beginning with a gradual increase in seize.

  b. Dodge Ball and similar games can be used to develop accuracy of throwing.

Catching

Keep the eyes on the ball throughout the catch. If the ball is thrown below the waist, catch it with the little fingers together and the fingers pointing down; if the ball is above the waist, the thumbs are together and the fingers point up. With each catch, bring the hands into the body and flex the knees to absorb the force.

 1. Start with large balls for success at short distances and gradually decrease the size of the ball and increase the distance. Use different colored balls and various weights for discrimination as well as catching skill.

 2. Ask "How far away can you catch a ball?" "How many balls can you catch at a short distance, a long distance?" "What is the best way for you to catch the ball?" "Which ball do you like to catch the best?" "Why?"

 3. Attach a ball overhead, swing it and let the individual catch it.

 4. Throw and catch with partners.

 5. Number game: Use groups of three or four and assign each individual a number. Throw a ball up in the air and call out a number. The person who has that number must catch the ball while it is in the air or on the first bounce.

Striking or Hitting

The striking activities involved in different sports represent a wide variety of skills. The implement may be the hand, as

136 *The Mentally Retarded Child and His Motor Behavior*

in handball; the foot, as in soccer; a short, solid paddle, as in table tennis; a racket, as in tennis; or, a solid stick or club as in baseball or golf. Several general principles apply to all striking activities. The length and weight of the implement used determine the speed and distance the struck object can be made to travel. The longer the lever and heavier the implement, the greater the force possible. The stance of the hitter at the time of impact will determine, to some extent, the direction of flight of the object. The nature of the flight of a struck object may be partly determined by the position of the striking implement on the object. An object struck in line with its

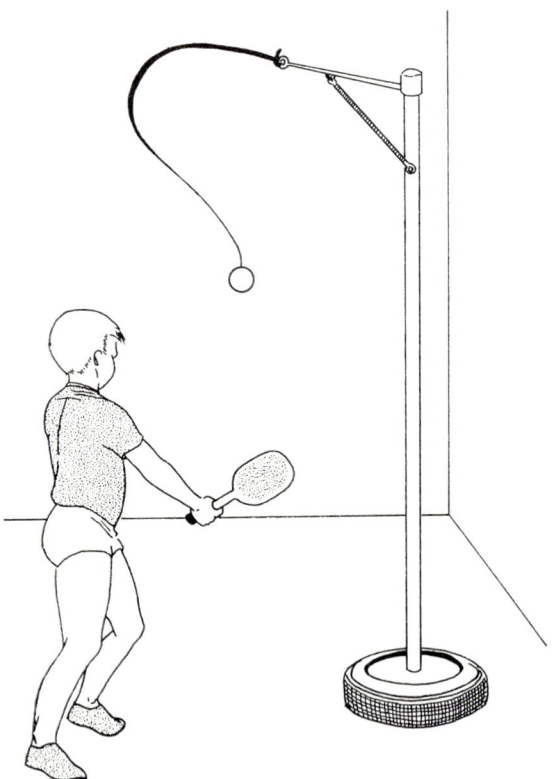

Figure 21. Striking apparatus.

center of gravity will tend to travel straight forward; below its center of gravity, backspin will be imparted; and, above its center of gravity, topspin will result.

Movement Experiences

Below are some suggestions for movement experiences.

1. Using rackets, paddles, plastic or wooden bats or just the hand, practice contacting a relatively stationary ball. Suspend a tennis ball from an overhead structure or an improvised post with a horizontal extension as shown in Figure 21. The individual should stand to the side and slightly behind the object to be struck, with the left side (if right-handed) facing in the direction of the hit ball. The knees should be flexed and the weight on the rear foot. As the implement is brought forward and the ball is contacted, the weight shifts from the rear to the forward foot. After the ball is contacted, the implement should continue to swing around the body in follow-through of the movement.

2. When the above movements are executed with success, the instructor should begin to throw various objects, utilized in specific game situations, to the individual. It is suggested that large balls be used in the beginning and that emphasis be placed on keeping the *eyes* on the ball or moving object.

Kicking

Similarities exist between kicking and striking activities and, therefore, the same principles apply to both. Use the broad surface of the foot and contact behind and slightly below the center of the ball.

1. Start by kicking large balls, from a stationary position, for both distance and height.

2. Kick at targets, under and over ropes for accuracy as well as height and distance.

3. Kick balls which are moving for accuracy, height and distance. Start by rolling the balls slowly, then increase the speed.

PERCEPTUAL-MOTOR EXPERIENCES
Body-Image

Once the individual has successfully indicated an awareness of the various parts of his body by identifying and locating them, you should proceed to movement experiences which give him an understanding of how these different parts of the body can be used in moving.

Identifying and Locating Body Parts

Some suggestions for locating and identifying body parts follow.

1. Utilizing commands similar to those given in Chapter 6, have the individual touch all of the parts of his body with the eyes open. *Example:* Verbal command is given, "Touch your knee/knees"; individual repeats the command and then touches that part of his body. Vary the body position (lying, standing, sitting).

2. Follow the same procedure as outlined in 1, but have the individual keep his eyes closed. Vary the body position.

3. Have the individual close his eyes. The instructor will then touch different parts of the person's body and he must respond verbally by saying, "You are touching my hand," and so forth.

4. Have two people work together as partners. One person will give the command, "Touch my shoulder," and the other person will respond verbally, "I am touching your shoulder," as he does so. This will aid in transferring the concepts of body parts to other people.

Movement Experiences for Understanding Use of Body Parts

Movement experiences to understand use of body parts are important.

1. Using the problem-solving approach, pose various ques-

tions to the individual or group which will aid in understanding the use of various body parts. Examples are as follow:

   a. What parts of your body are used to stand like a horse or a dog?
   b. Can you stand on your chest? Show me. What can you do with your chest?
   c. Are you able to place your shoulder against the wall? Show me.
   d. Can you run on your knees? Show me.
   e. Can you turn your head around? Which way did you turn? Can you see your back?
   f. Can you touch the lower part of your leg/legs without bending your knees? How?
   g. Can you touch both of your legs at the same time? How?
   h. Can you touch your elbows together? How?
   i. With how many different parts of your body can you touch your stomach?
   j. What parts of your body are small, large, short, long?

2. Using balloons, have the person hit the balloon up in the air with the hands first, then ask him to keep it up by hitting it with a different part of the body each time.

Laterality

As previously mentioned in Chapter 6, laterality and body awareness are very closely related. Many body parts are paired and are on opposite sides of the body. The authors feel that the logical progression is from body awareness to laterality in terms of major emphasis placed on the results expected. Many of the same movement experiences suggested for developing body awareness, however, can also be used for developing laterality. The only difference would be to emphasize the *left* and *right* body part or segment. We suggest, therefore, that the following previously outlined activities be used for developing laterality:

1. Chapter 6, "*Verbal Commands.*"
2. Chapter 7, "*Static and Dynamic Balance.*"
3. The experiences described under "Body-Image" in the previous section.
4. Once the individual exhibits a firmly established concept of right and left, we suggest that time be spent with the movement experiences described in Chapter 6 under "Laterality and Midline."

It has been pointed out before that laterality is an internal awareness of left and right. For this reason, the authors feel that the kinesthetic sense is an important modality for developing laterality and suggest that a major emphasis be placed on kinesthetic awareness in all of the movement experiences presented in this section.

Directionality

When a body-image and internal awareness of left and right have been developed, the individual is ready to start transferring this knowledge to his external world of space. He must be given many and varied opportunities to recognize and perceive objects in space as being located on his right, left, above him, below him, in front and in back of him.

The authors suggest that developmental experiences for directionality be kept fairly simple in the beginning.

Exploration of External Space

Exploration of external space can be aided in the following ways:

1. From a seated position in any kind of room, have the individual simply name three objects that are on his right side, left side, in front of him, in back of him.
2. Have the person move to and touch objects to his right, left, in front and in back of him. As he moves and touches the objects, have him verbalize, "This book is on my right," and so forth.
3. Have the person move to an object on his right, pick it up

Movement to Develop Perceptual-Motor Efficiency 141

and change its position so that it is now on his left side. As he goes through the movement, have him verbalize his actions.

Games Involving Directionality

Several games are described below which involve directionality.

1. Place targets of any kind on a wall so that one is to the right, left, up and down as shown in Figure 22. Using a ball, darts or any suitable object, have the person throw the object to the target called out by the instructor. For example, have him throw to the target on his left, right, top, bottom. Then have the individual give himself the command, "I am going to throw to the top target, right target," and so on.

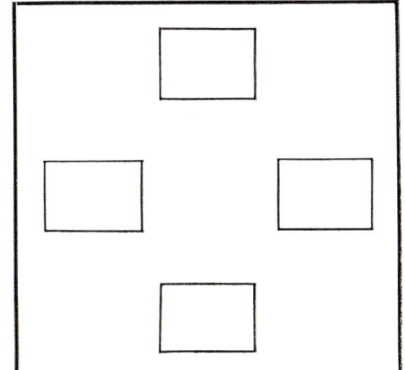

Figure 22. Directionality wall targets.

2. Beter-Cragin bean bag test: The test and the modification described in Chapter 6 can also be used as developmental activities.

3. Ball activities: Using various kinds of balls, tires, chairs or a partner, have the individual roll, throw or kick the ball to prescribed directions. For example, throw the ball to the right side of the tire, roll the ball under the chair, kick the ball to the left of your partner, and so forth.

4. Beter-Cragin oral directions-motor response test: The test described in Chapter 6, with similar modifications added, can be used for developing directionality.

Directionality Involving Multisensory Modalities

In addition to developmental experiences which involve the visual sense, activities should also be used which require the auditory, tactile and kinesthetic senses.

1. Auditory: Check directionality by having the individual identify the direction of various sounds. For example, using a tambourine or similar instrument, move around the individual and have him identify the direction of the sound while keeping his eyes closed.

2. Tactile: Place dissimilar objects to the right, left, front and back of the individual. Keeping the eyes closed, ask the individual to tell you what is on his right side by feeling it.

3. Kinesthetic: With the eyes closed, have the individual perform various movements involving different directions. Examples are the following:
    a. Stoop down as close to the floor as possible.
    b. Raise your body up as high as you can.
    c. Slide to your right, to your left.
    d. Walk forward, then backward.

Temporal-Spatial Relationships

As explained in Chapter 6, the authors have chosen to use the single word *rhythm* to refer to that aspect of human behavior which involves the organization of time and space events. We agree with the interpretation of Mead[48] that "Whenever events are organized in space, in time, or in space-time, and provided that the organization of events can be recognized and repeated, there is rhythm." This broad interpretation of rhythm means that we are considering the organization of visual, auditory and proprioceptive stimuli as an important part of the total perceptual process and feel, therefore, that it plays a vital role in the learning process. In the organization of auditory stimuli, for instance, the tick of a clock or any other steady beat measures time into intervals. Perception of sounds and the intervals which occur between sounds, then, can help in developing an awareness of time. When an auditory stimulus is perceived at the approximate time it is being received, we become conscious of the present; a sound event which is heard and later recalled is perceived as the past, and anticipating the next sound event in a pattern helps us to conceive of the future. Much of our external environment represents the rhythmic structure of visual stimuli in much the same way as sound events are organized. The facade of a modern building gives us an example of visual rhythmic structure. The endless rows of windows which we perceive as a rhythmic structure are such because the steel girders have been placed in such a manner as to accent units of what would otherwise be a continuous piece of glass. In the case of both auditory and visual rhythmic structures, the order of the structure (accent, emphasis or beat) is superimposed upon the individual. That is, if an individual perceives a waltz as anything but a 1-2-3 rhythm, he would be judged as lacking auditory rhythm in this case. If he perceives the modern building as having a continuous facade of glass, he is unable to perceive a visual rhythmic structure. The authors pointed out previously that a great deal more research has to be done in the area of rhythm, but a basic assumption seems tenable that the above concept of rhythm has a relationship to learning activities such as reading and writing.

The third type of rhythmic structure which needs to be considered is proprioceptive. This involves the organization of body-movement events. This type of rhythmic experience can result in a superimposed rhythmic structure, or the organization of rhythmic events can be determined by the performer. Movement experiences such as dance or precision marching would constitute superimposed structure. Movement experiences such as sports activities, however, offer an opportunity for self-determined rhythmic organization.

Based on this rather brief discussion of rhythm, we would point out that the aspect of rhythm is inherent in all of the movement experiences which have already been presented in other sections of this book. Specific activities, designed to emphasize rhythm, should also be used and these activities should include opportunities for structured rhythmic experiences as well as free, creative rhythmic exploration.

Structured Activities

The following list provides examples of structured activities.

1. Orientation to auditory rhythmic structures.
    a. Using a metronome, bongo drum, tin can or tambourine, introduce various rhythmic structures and have the students keep time by clapping their hands, slapping the knee or patting a foot. Progress from a steady "da-da-da-da" beat to "da-dit" to "da-dit-dit." Emphasize not only the different beats, but also the accent between beats in a sequence. Also include various tempos.
    b. Once the individuals are capable of recognizing beats, accents and tempos, let them follow different rhythms with their own instruments. If records are used for the background music, the instructor will be free to move around and give individual help. Rhythm sticks, coffee cans with plastic tops or any suitable instrument can be used by the students.
    c. Gradually increase the degree of total body movement as the individuals become more adept at recognizing various rhythms. Let them hop, walk, run, leap, slide and gallop to the various beats.

2. Orientation to visual rhythmic structures: Since multisensory stimuli are important in all learning experiences for children with educational difficulties, special emphasis should be given to the organization of visual cues into rhythmic structures.
    a. Using simple charts, which can be devised by the reader, have the individual follow a progression as described in the section for auditory rhythms. The

charts are shown to the individual and he beats out the appropriate rhythm, or moves to it as suggested in the previous section. A steady "da-da-da" beat could be shown visually as illustrated in the top row of Figure 23. The middle row of the same figure represents the presentation of a "da-dit" beat; a "da-dit-dit" beat is shown in the bottom row.

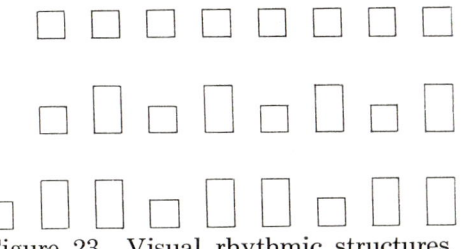

Figure 23. Visual rhythmic structures.

3. Orientation to proprioceptive rhythmic structures: The organization of proprioceptive stimuli will occur in connection with the movement activities suggested in the progression for auditory and visual structured activities. In addition to the locomotor movement experiences, opportunity should also be provided for axial movements. These would involve such things as twisting, bending, stretching, changing body position from standing, lying, kneeling or sitting.

Unstructured or Creative Movement Experiences

Although it is important in the developmental learning process for mentally retarded children to learn to recognize predetermined rhythmic patterns, they also need opportunities for creative movement exploration to various rhythms. So often these individuals are treated as automatons who are expected to respond only to directions and commands. They are fully capable, however, of creating and they need opportunities to use this ability and to build their confidence. Therefore, some portion of the program set aside for rhythmic experiences should involve unstructured movement. Some guidance and encouragement may be necessary in the beginning, but the individual should be gradually brought to the point where he depends entirely upon his own instincts and feelings for the movement performed. Simple body movements incorporating basic locomotor skills (hopping, skipping, and so on) or axial movements (twisting, bending) can be suggested at the start. As confidence is built up, the individuals should be encouraged to include balls, ropes or wands as part of the movement they create to various rhythm patterns.

Sensory Efficiency

At the core of the overall problem for so many children with educational difficulties is usually a combination of perceptual impairment in one or more sense areas and a general deprivation of total sensory experiences.

It is the opinion of these authors that mentally retarded children need a wide variety of experiences which require the use of all sense modalities, and we have included this section on sensory efficiency for that reason. We agree with Kephart[39] that the perceptual process cannot be broken down into isolated parts; it operates as a totality. In this sense, then, learning experiences presented for developing an isolated sense modality would normally serve little purpose. Since the integrative process involves past experiences and multisensory stimuli, however, it is important that these children build their experiential background.

In all of the learning experiences presented thus far, the authors have suggested a multisensory approach. For individuals who obviously lack sensory experiences, we suggest that time be spent in some of the activities presented in Chapter 6.

Perceptuo-Scope

The perceptuo-scope is a developmental learning device designed and utilized by the authors in the program at their private school of perceptual-motor development. It is being included at the end of this chapter because it offers an opportunity for a variety of educational experiences directly related to perceptual efficiency.

Description

Geometric symbols, letters of the alphabet and numbers as they appear on the face of the clock are painted on the floor as shown in Figure 24. The numbers on the face of the clock form the inside of a large circle and the letters and geometric symbols are painted around the outer part of the clock.

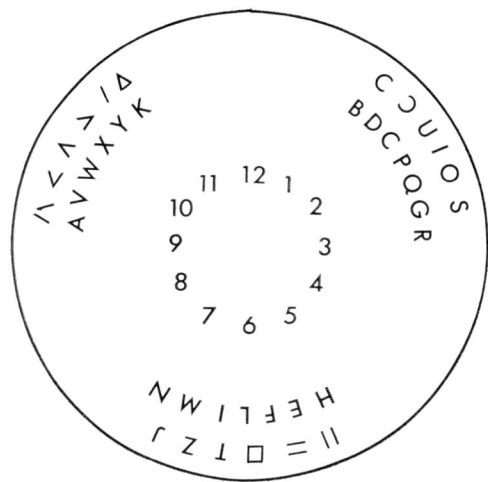

Figure 24. Beter-Cragin Perceptuo-Scope.

Developmental Experiences

The perceptuo-scope was designed to be used for a variety of activities and to utilize multisensory modalities. The letters have been grouped according to their relationships with the circle, square and triangle, and the parts of these geometric figures are also presented. Different colors can be used for each group of letters to help distinguish them and also to aid in learning colors. Some suggestions for using the perceptuo-scope are given below.

1. Simple letter, symbol, number and color recognition. Word formation and vocabulary.
   a. Throw a ball or bean bag to various letters, numbers or symbols upon command from the instructor. Throw from self-commands.

  b. Use locomotor movements (walk, hop, jump) to identify letters, symbols or numbers and to form words.
2. Telling time.
  a. Use a rope or large piece of string as the hands of the clock and move the hands around to form different hours, half hours, and so forth.
  b. Have the student use his own legs as the hands of the clock and move them around to different times. Have him lie on the floor and use his arms as the hands of the clock.

The above suggestions represent only a sample of the many activities which can be devised, and we encourage the readers to use their own innovations.

SELECTED READINGS

1. Reading Research Foundation, Inc.: *Perceptual-Motor Training.* Chicago, 1969.
2. Chaney, Clara M., and Kephart, Newell C.: *Motoric Aids to Perceptual Training.* Columbus, Merrill, 1968.

Chapter 9

SOCIAL PATTERNS OF BEHAVIOR AND LEISURE-TIME ACTIVITIES

Come on over—let's play.
—ULRICH

SOCIAL PATTERNS OF BEHAVIOR

ACCORDING TO ULRICH,[76] when one individual says to another, "Come on over—let's play," he is erecting the framework for the most fundamental and most meaningful *interaction* possible. Although the invitation to play is universal, it is uniquely unencumbered with the usual social stigmata of age limits, language barriers, socioeconomic limitations or status overtones. Play, as a medium for social interaction, has certain assets and liabilities which could be expected from any human intercourse; yet, it encompasses a richness of behavioral experiences and concomitant learnings that are unequaled in any other situation. Play exists, therefore it is; and, as such, it has no allegiance to any cause other than creating its own world of moving, feeling, reacting, perceiving and becoming.

Authorities in the behavioral sciences acknowledge that play is one of the basic needs of man, but there are a variety of theories offered as to why the need exists. Some of the theories suggest a physiological basis for the need, others a psychological basis, and still others favor a sociological basis. Understanding the basis for the need to play is really not as important as recognizing that such a need exists and realizing that the need is as strong for the mentally retarded child as it is for any other individual.

A number of research studies have been conducted to investigate certain relationships of play and the social and and emotional adjustment of mentally retarded children. Smith and Hurst[69] concluded, in their study of trainable and educable mentally retarded children, that motor ability plays a significant role in peer acceptance. Oliver[54] reported an improvement in the emotional adjustment of mentally retarded boys after they had participated in a ten-week period of concentrated physical training. A comparison of emotional adjustment with levels of intelligence in 120 fourth-grade public school children was made by Enos.[25] He found that the superior group of girls made the best adjustment and the educable mentally retarded girls were the most maladjusted. In an earlier study by Kennedy,[38] findings indicated that retardates between the ages of twenty and thirty participated to a lesser extent in group and recreational activities than did the nonretarded group. In a more recent study, McDaniel[46] investigated the effect of participation in the extracurricular activities of basketball and square dancing upon social acceptance among educable mentally retarded students. The findings indicated that social acceptance increased with time among those who participated in the extracurricular activities, and that social rejection increased among the control group which did not have the extracurricular program. In discussing the implications of his study, McDaniel stated that ". . . comprehensive extracurricular activities programs must be designed to play important parts in the academic education of educable mentally retarded students."

As Kirk[40] pointed out, there is no difference in the basic social traits between educable mentally retarded and average children. Although it is not uncommon to hear people correlate delinquency and antisocial behavior with mental retardation, the picture is much more complex than this simple correlation suggests. A high percentage of children who are classified as mentally retarded come from the low socioeconomic segment of society. Delinquent behavior among this group could as justifiably be attributed to the substandard environment in which they live as it could be attributed to their intellectual functioning. The authors feel that the important factor to be considered in relation to social behavior of retardates is the relationship between acceptable behavior and the ego, or total personality development of the individual. Behavior problems have traditionally been known to result when there is a conflict between the individual's ability to perform and the demands placed upon him by his environment. This conflict is particularly prevalent in the lives of retardates.

The authors have observed through teaching and research experiences with children who have educational difficulties that when they are given a task commensurate with their abilities wherein success is self-evident from the performance, desirable social and emotional attributes occur. For everyone, success is built upon success and frustrations are built upon frustrations. The highest score in any situation is the winning score, which when totaled includes success, motivation, confidence, skill, social adjustment, self-esteem and a feeling of worth.

As previously mentioned, the building of desirable social behavior and emotional stability is an integral part of the emerging personality or self. The self-concept, or one's feelings about himself, determines to a very large extent how the individual will behave. We know that the self-concept is an ongoing process of experiencing and evaluating and that it involves a bank account of feelings about a variety of things. A very important item in the collection is the feeling a person has about his physical appearance and his capacity to perform motor tasks. Proficiency in sports and his physique have always been important determinants of self-confidence in the male; and, the development of a figure which resembles the acceptable norm has always been of great importance to the female. It seems logical to assume, therefore, that these variables would be equally important in the total self-concept of retardates.

Using a survey form of self-reports adapted by Cratty,[19] the authors assessed the opinions of nineteen teen-age male and female retardates concerning physical appearance and motor performance. Scores were obtained by the individual's Yes or No response to the items listed (see Appendix). Some of the questions pertaining to motor performance which elicited responses indicating a negative self-concept were "Are you strong?" "Are you the last to be chosen for games?" "Are you clumsy?" "In games do you watch instead of play?" Responses to questions concerning physical appearance such as "Are you handsome/pretty?" "Do you wish you were different?" also indicated negative self-concepts.

It seems evident from this limited sampling that retarded children are as normal as any other individual in relating their own physical appearance and motor performance to what they apparently are able to recognize as the *acceptable norm*. Certainly this is not conclusive evidence, but it adds another pillar of support for the contention that provision *must* be made for educational experiences which will aid in developing a more positive self-concept. The authors have been particularly interested in this aspect of educating children with learning difficulties and our day-to-day experiences only serve to reinforce the belief that this is a major catalyst in the learning environment.

Participation in leisure-time sports activities provides a desirable social avenue for the retarded child to interact with his own peers and also with the more typical individual. More importantly, the retardate *can* develop proficiency in motor skills and when success prevails and is realized, he will be encouraged to participate further. Through a carefully planned and implemented program of leisure-time skills and activities, the retarded child will be afforded an opportunity to build a positive self-concept, to socially interact and to further enhance his perceptual-motor development, which in turn can be conducive to additional learning and cognitive growth.

SPORTS, RHYTHMS AND GAMES FOR LEISURE-TIME ENJOYMENT

Included in this section are sports, rhythms and games for leisure-time enjoyment which the authors have found to be particularly applicable in programs for children with learning difficulties. Although some individuals will need a great deal of assistance and will have to proceed at a slower pace, we do not feel that special modifications of the activities need to be made. Since it would be impractical to include coverage of each sport, game and dance in its entirety, this section contains suggestions for appropriate activities and the selected skills that should be included. Where it was appropriate, we have also included suggestions for improvised equipment and special recommendations about teaching the skills. There are numerous references which include full details about these activities and we have included a list of these at the end of the chapter.

Limited group demonstration and verbal instructions should be given for each of the following activities. As previously suggested in Chapter 8, all skills should be taught from a simple, concrete approach and should progress to complex skills as success and improvement are evidenced. In activities of a *dual* nature, individuals of like ability should be engaged as opponents. In activities of a *team* nature, the authors have observed from experience that it is advisable to alternate team members periodically. This, of course, is left to the discretion of the instructor and depends upon the individuals in the group and the class situation. Class tournaments for appropriate activities are suggested as a culminating feature to enhance competition within the group, as well as self-competition for each person.

Leisure-Time Individual Sports Activities

Selected Skills of Angling

Skills: Bait casting and aiming.
Materials: Rod, reel, line, lure and target are used. Old tires are good for targets, and a light weight, rather than an expensive lure is suggested.

Selected Skills of Archery

Skills: Stance, scoring, nocking, drawing the bow, aiming, releasing and retrieving the arrow.

Materials: If they are available, it is desirable to use bows of various weights and arrows of different lengths. For teaching the beginning skills to children who have never had an opportunity to shoot, however, inexpensive commercial sets can be used. Targets can be made from cloth or cardboard and placed between two poles in the ground or tacked on a frame. For *clout* shooting, the target is drawn on the ground, using large circles, and the arrow is shot into the air from a distance of twenty yards from the target.

In the beginning, allow the individuals to shoot at relatively short distances for success and to acquire the feel of drawing the bow (force). If the individual desires to shoot the bow in a horizontal rather than a vertical position, let him do so if success is being achieved. After a reasonable amount of time, allow the individuals to see how far they can shoot the arrow.

Selected Skills of Badminton

Skills: Underhand and overhead clears, smash, singles and doubles, rules and scoring.

Materials: Inexpensive commercial badminton sets can be used to teach beginners. If this is not available, rackets can be made by stretching nylon hose over coat hangers bent in the shape of a badminton racket. Ropes can be stretched between two posts and the court dimensions can be modified for any available area.

Dropping the birdie and contacting it with the underhand clear, the stroke used for serving, is often quite difficult for these children to accomplish. If they are having difficulty, allow them to put the birdie in play by placing it, feathers down, on the racket face and swinging the racket arm forward. When they have accomplished the drop and hit, additional practice can be obtained by continuous stroking of the birdie up in the air, or by continuous stroking against a wall.

Selected Skills of Bowling

Skills: Grip, approach, delivery, scoring and aiming.

Materials: It is not necessary to have access to a regular bowling alley to teach bowling. Milk cartons, plastic bottles, cans or wooden blocks can be used for the pins and a softball or any ball heavy enough to exert force can be used.

Selected Skills of Golf
Skills: Grip, stance, driving, iron stroking and putting.
Materials: Regular golf clubs would naturally be desirable. If they are not available, however, wooden sticks with club heads cut at various angles could be constructed for stroking. Plastic balls can be used both inside and outdoors if the area is limited. A very effective putting course can be constructed by using blocks of wood, bean bags, tin cans with both ends cut out, and so forth for the holes.

Selected Skills of Tennis
Skills: Grip, stance, forehand and backhand drives, serve, scoring and rules.
Materials: A makeshift court can be used by modifying the court for any available area and stretching a rope between two posts. Strokes can be practiced by hitting against a wall or side of a building.

Selected Skills of Swimming
Beginning Skills: Breath holding, rhythmic breathing, jellyfish float, prone float, prone and back glide, finning, flutter kick, elementary backstroke, changing positions and directions, jumping into the water, treading, the American crawl and underwater swimming.
Intermediate Skills: Breaststroke, sidestroke, back crawl, turns, diving from the one- and three-meter springbroads.

Leisure-Time Team Sports Activities
Selected Skills of Basketball
Skills: Dribbling, passing (chest, one- and two-hand overhead pass), shooting (free throws, lay-up shots and push-shots), and guarding.

Selected Skills of Football (Touch)
Skills: Kicking, catching, tagging, passing, centering the ball and blocking.

Selected Skills of Gator Ball
Skills: This is a team sport (six or more on each team) involving a combination of the skills of touch football, soccer, and basketball. In addition to the skills already given for basketball and football, the students would need skills for dribbling with alternate feet, partner dribbling, place (drop) kicking, catching, jump balls and trapping the ball with the feet.

In the beginning of the learning period, utilize an area about half the size of a football field.

Selected Skills of Field Hockey
Skills: Dribbling, driving, tackling, bullying and scoring.
Materials: Wooden hockey sticks, softballs or tennis balls are used.
Broom Hockey: This is played according to the same rules as field hockey, but can be played indoors and on a smaller area. Old brooms, cut to fit the size of the players, and small wooden discs are used to play the game.

Selected Skills of Softball
Skills: Gripping, batting, catching, throwing, pitching and fielding.
Materials: In addition to regular bats and balls, plastic bats and balls can be used for individuals having difficulty contacting the ball and also for indoor use.
Kick Ball: This is played with the same rules as softball, but a soccer ball is used and is kicked instead of being hit. Another variation which is helpful in teaching beginners is to have the person at bat catch the ball and throw it into the field immediately instead of batting or kicking it.

Selected Skills of Volleyball
Skills: Serving, setting up, spiking and retrieving from the net.
Bounce Ball: This game is played the same as volleyball except the net is lowered to about waist-height and the ball is allowed to bounce and then is hit. To serve, you also bounce the ball and then hit it.

Leisure-Time Recreational Games

Selected Skills of Dart Throwing
Skills: Throwing and aiming.
Materials: In addition to a regular dartboard, targets can be made from cardboard or cloth with various designs and numbers.

Selected Skills of Deck Tennis
Skills: Grip, catch, serve and return.
Materials: A rope stretched between two posts and plastic or rubber rings from a ring-toss game can be used in place of a regular desk tennis set.

Selected Skills of Horseshoe Pitching
Skills: Grip, stance, throwing, aiming and scoring.

Selected Skills of Ping-Pong®
Skills: Grip, forehand and backhand strokes, scoring and rules for singles and doubles.
Materials: A piece of plywood placed over two sidehorses or a trampoline can be used if a regular Ping-Pong table is not available.

Selected Skills of Shuffleboard
Skills: Aim, stance and delivery.

Leisure-Time Rhythms Activities

Skills: Forward, backward and sideward steps and balance movements.
Dances: Waltz, fox-trot, cha-cha and contemporary variations.

Selected Square Dance Skills

Skills: Allemande left and right, break, circle, do-si-do-, square promenade (Western), separate, swing, line and balance.

Dances: Square Dance Fair, Promenade and Do-Si-Do, and *Square Dance Fun Festival.* These are suggested types of dances which do not require too many complicated instructions.

Selected Folk Dance Skills

Skills: Circle left and circle right, forward, backward, sideward and center movements.

Dances: Dancing Round the World, Folk Dance Festival, and *Dances of Many Lands.*

Stick Dancing (Tinikling): Two or four bambo poles are used and struck together in steady rhythm while the dancers leap or jump between the poles as they separate. The dance can be done individually or with partners.

Sock It! Block It!

This game was developed by the authors and cannot be found in other references for sports activities. Since we feel that it is particularly appropriate for children with learning problems, we are including all of the necessary details about the game. Aside from being a lot of fun to play, the game is especially beneficial in developing reaction time, agility and endurance. It can also be used effectively in developing laterality and directionality.

Materials Needed: The game was originally designed to be played on a trampoline, which already has the four pockets and playing surface. If a trampoline is not available, a similar area can be constructed by stretching a piece of canvas, net or other material which can be pulled taut over a frame, and then cutting out pockets at either side of each end. The game is played with a volleyball or rubber playground ball (size dependent upon the age and ability of the players). The size of the playing court can vary according to equipment available. The trampoline on which the game was developed has a frame which is six feet wide and ten feet long, and we feel that this should be a minimum size.

Playing Procedure Singles (Two Players): One player is situated at either end of the playing court, midway between the two scoring pockets on his side. The winner of a coin toss puts the ball in play to start the game by socking it with one or both hands, or by rolling it across the playing court, in an attempt to get it into one of the scoring pockets on his opponent's end of the court. If the ball is approaching a pocket, the opponent attempts to *block* it and keep it from going into the pocket; he then rolls or *socks* the ball back across the court in an attempt to get it into the pocket on his opponent's side. The game continues in this manner until one of the two players scores *ten points*. Each time a point is made, the player who was scored against puts the ball into play. If the ball rolls off the playing surface, the first player to retrieve it can put it into play from his end of the court. As the ball is being played back and forth, the player may hit it back as he blocks it, or the ball may be caught and put in play by hitting or socking it with either or both hands each time it comes to a player's end of the court. In an attempt to block the ball, a point is scored even when the defensive player unwillfully adds impetus to the ball as it falls into the pocket.

Playing Procedure Doubles (Four Players): Two players are situated at either end of the court as in singles and their partners are situated midway at either side of the court. The ball is put into play to start the game by the end player of the side winning the toss. The game is played the same as described for singles, with the following exceptions:

1. Twenty points terminate the game.
2. The two side players can intercept the ball at any time, block it on their end of the court, and can score by socking the ball into the opponent's pocket from the side position of the court.
3. A ball which rolls off the playing court can be retrieved by one of the side players and put in play from the side position.

Balls put into play after a score must be from the end position of the court.

Modifications:

1. For very unskilled players, it would be advisable to use a ball slightly larger than a volleyball and to start with the doubles game.

2. For highly skilled players, a more advanced version of the game can be played by throwing the ball into the pockets instead of rolling or socking it.

SELECTED READINGS

1. Fait, Hollis, et al.: Angling. In *A Manual of Physical Education Activities*. Philadelphia, Saunders.
2. *Sports Series: Archery, Badminton, Bowling, Field Hockey, Golf, Soccer, Social Dance, Softball, Swimming, Table Tennis, Women's and Men's Basketball, Tennis and Volleyball*. Dubuque, W. C. Brown.
3. Stanley and Waglow: Gator ball, Touch football, Deck tennis, Horseshoe pitching, Tabble tennis, Shuffleboard, Social, square and folk dance. In *Physical Education Activities*. Boston, Allyn & Bacon.
4. Tinikling. In *Dance*. New York, McKay, Sole Educational Distributor.

Chapter 10

THREE SELECTED CASE STUDIES

Movement *is* what movement *does*.

—BETER

INTRODUCTION: WHERE AM I GOING?

I AM GOING where practical, meaningful objectives can be attained through an understanding of the individuals guiding my experiences toward self-fulfillment. Start me where I am: to learn to move so I move to learn.

The understanding necessary to plan and guide experiences of young people toward self-fulfillment is one that has its roots deeply embedded in many aspects of human development and behavior. In planning and guiding experiences for the mentally retarded child, the authors feel that two very important building blocks are an understanding of *self* and an understanding of *movement*.

We start by remembering that that which is *self*, to be ultimately freed for maximum growth, must be accepted as that of its current structure.[4] Remembering, also, that the self is a unified organism, we turn our attention to the function of movement in the development of that unified organism. According to Whitehurst,[79] the significance of the motor dimension in the development of young children has long been recognized. She further points out that movement has come to play a very meaningful role for the child therapist and the developmental psychologist in helping to analyze and understand both normal and abnormal behavior. More importantly, Whitehurst interprets for us the meaning of movement from the viewpoint of the child himself. To the child, movement means life, self-discovery, physical and social environmental discovery, spatial and self-expressive freedom, safety, communication, enjoyment, sensuous pleasure and acceptance.

Movement is playing, movement is learning, movement is doing. Because we recognize and respect the individuality of the self, we know that the needs and interests of individuals will vary. There are many children for whom movement experiences will represent only one of many roads toward achieving self-fulfillment. For others, movement may be the *prime mover* in kindling the spark of interest and motivation for achieving other aspects of development. Then there are those for whom movement experiences will be the *only* way for achieving self-fulfillment.

CASE STUDIES

This section will include three individual case studies of students who were enrolled in the authors' private school of perceptual-motor development for a period of nine months. The primary purpose of the case studies is to illustrate the use of various movement experiences, presented in previous chapters, in planning a program for different individuals. Each student's program of educational experiences is presented as the person engaged in them throughout the nine-month period. None of the three individuals had had any previous concentrated program of physical education on a daily basis.

A complete evaluation was made of each student after establishing the rapport necessary for mutual trust and confidence. The evaluation for each student included the recording of age, height, weight and body type and posture assessment. Other tests administered included the following:

Modified Harvard Step Test (cardiovascular efficiency).
Modified Sit and Reach Test (flexibility).
Sit-ups, Push-ups, Flexed Bar Hang (muscular endurance.)
Spring Scale Press and Curl (muscular strength).
Side Step Test and Quadrant Jump (agility).
Nelson Balance Test (static and dynamic balance).
Standing Broad Jump (muscular power).

Horizontal and Vertical Linear Space Tests, Distance Perception Jump (kinesthetic perception).
Nelson Reaction Time Test (reaction time).
Harvey Rhythm Test (rhythm).
Tests for Perceptual-Motor Efficiency (see Ch. 6).
The Gates-McGinitie Reading Tests.
Wide Range Achievement Tests.
Illinois Tests of Psycholinguistic Abilities.
Bender-Gestalt Visual Motor Test.
Cratty's Adapted Self-Opinion Survey.

Student 1

Student 1 was a seventeen-year-old male Caucasian. This student has been subject to both grand mal and petit mal seizures since the age of three, has severe cerebral dysfunction which is manifested in visual, auditory and kinesthetic perceptual difficulties and motor dysfunction. At the time he enrolled, body-image, laterality, directionality and temporal-spatial relationships had not been established; he was a nonreader. His previous educational experiences had been encountered primarily through private schools and tutors. This student was enrolled in the program for a two-hour session five days a week.

Movement Experiences (First–Third Months)

Locomotor: The problem-solving situations and degrees of variation (as described in Ch. 8) were used for each movement.

1. Walking: Forward, backward, fast and slow.
2. Jumping: Vertically and horizontally.
3. Hopping: For distance and height, forward and backward.

Basic Motor Skills.

1. Throwing: Large colored balls and bean bags were thrown underarm and overarm at short distances.
2. Catching: Large balls of various colors were used at short distances.

3. Striking or hitting: Used the hand to contact relatively stationary balls.

Physiological Efficiency-Interval Training: The full description of each movement, variation and problem-solving situation can be found in Chapter 7.

1. Muscular strength.
   a. Used a rope, horizontal bar and weight lifting for arms and shoulders.
   b. Sit-ups for the abdomen.
   c. Used a rope, broad jump and duck walk for the legs.
2. Muscular endurance.
   a. Squat jumps for the legs.
   b. Sit-ups for the abdomen.
   c. Push-ups and crab walk for the arms and shoulders.
3. Flexibility.
   a. Lower back and leg stretch.
   b. Shoulder extension.
   c. Trunk extension.
4. Cardiovascular endurance.
   a. Movements described under muscular strength and muscular endurance were performed without a rest in a relatively short period of time.
5. Relaxation.
   a. Head and neck.
   b. Shoulders.
   c. Arms.
   d. Trunk.
   e. Legs.
6. Posture.
   a. Lower neck and upper back strengthening.
7. Balance.
   a. Static—foot and knee balance.
   b. Dynamic—walking the blocks and beam used for the Nelson Balance Test.

All of the above movements involved the use of verbal commands as described in Chapter 7.

Perceptual-Motor Efficiency.

1. Body-image.
    a. Identifying and locating body parts from verbal commands.
2. Laterality.
    a. Verbal commands requiring movement of specific body segments.
    b. Balance, both static and dynamic.
3. Laterality-midline.
    a. Verbal commands requiring movements that involved crossing the midline of the body.
    b. Balance, both static and dynamic.
4. Directionality.
    a. Exploration of external space.
    b. Beter-Cragin Bean Bag Test
    c. Ball activities.
    d. Beter-Cragin Oral Directions-Motor Response Checklist.
    e. Directionality activities involving the tactile, auditory and kinesthetic senses.
5. Temporal relationships.
    a. Creative movement experiences.
6. Sensory efficiency.
    a. Beter-Cragin Perceptuo-Scope.

Selected Skills of Sports and Recreational Games.

1. Archery.
2. Dart throwing.
3. Basketball: Dribbling, shooting the two-hand shot from short distances and catching the rebound.

Problem-solving situations, laterality and directionality were also incorporated into the sports skills movement experiences. *Parent Conference and Progress Report.* At the end of the three-month period, improvement was indicated in all areas. Both the number and duration of seizures had been reduced at the school and at home. The student displayed a desire and willingness to learn, and motivation was extremely high. Concentration and attention span were noticed to have significantly increased since his enrollment. Self-confidence and self-concept were notably in a more positive direction.

Movement and Other Educational Experiences (Fourth–Sixth Months)

Locomotor.

1. All movements as previously mentioned were engaged in with increased degrees of difficulty introduced, number of repetitions of movements increased, and the time intervals decreased.
2. Combinations of locomotor movements were engaged in.
3. Running relatively short distances, combined with other locomotor movements.
4. More time was devoted to exploratory and creative movements.

Basic Motor Skills.

1. Same motor skills mentioned previously with increasing difficulty.
2. Introduction of kicking.

Physiological Efficiency.

1. Previously described movements with increased difficulty.
2. More emphasis on agility and balance.

Perceptual-Motor Efficiency.

1. Movement experiences for understanding the use of body parts.
2. All movements described in the one to three-month section, under each heading, with increased difficulty.
3. Temporal relationships as described in Chapter 8 under "structured activities."

Selected Skills of Sports and Recreational Games.

1. Archery, dart throwing and basketball with increased degrees of difficulty.
2. Ring toss.
3. Card playing.
4. Horseshoe pitching.
5. Putting.

Other Selected Educational Experiences.

1. Letters painted on the top of large bottle caps were used for letter recognition.
2. These bottle caps were also placed by the student in a wooden frame to emphasize the concept of reading from left to right. Simple words were used and the student was required to place the letters in the frame to get the idea of the beginning and ending of words. The sounds of the letters were also emphasized with this activity.
3. Typing was introduced as further training in transferring letters and keeping the proper left-to-right sequence.
4. An audiotape, "Movement through the Alphabet," which was developed by the authors, was also introduced. Each letter of the alphabet is sounded and followed by references to certain types of movement. For example, "B, balance, badminton"; a relatively short question regarding movement followed. For example, "Can you balance on the right or left foot?" This tape was played every other day for a month.

Parent Conference and Progress Report. Following the six-month period, temporal-spatial relationships appeared, laterality and directionality were more firmly established, cursive letter writing and connecting two letters improved, word recognition and sound discrimination were better and progress was made in all physiological areas. The student's seizures had diminished to only two during this period at the school and they occurred less frequently in the home.

Movement and Other Educational Experiences (Seventh–Ninth Months)

Activity during this period is summarized below.

1. All movements as previously described under all sections were continued and the degree of difficulty was continuously increased by combining movements and making them more complex.

2. Social dancing was introduced along with bag punching. Also introduced was throwing balls through a swinging tire.

3. Circuit and interval training were used with movement experiences for developing physiological efficiency, and the student was given more responsibility for exercising on his own.

4. Copying sentences from various textbooks was used to continue practice in letter sequence and visual attention span.

Parent Conference and Progress Report. Improvement continued to be shown in all areas. The student was now able to recognize words at the 1.8 grade level. He could read short sentences written on cards; he could tell time on the hour and could recall days of the week more readily, although still with some difficulty. His temporal-spatial relationships continued to improve and his conversation was much more rational and organized. Only one seizure occurred at the school during this period and they were still occurring less frequently at home. The student was reported to be engaging in more movement activities at home; his social interaction in groups was improved and he generally had a more positive attitude toward learning and living.

Student 2

Student 2 was a twenty-year-old female Caucasian with Downs syndrome. Evaluation at the time of enrollment indicated difficulty in the auditory, visual and temporal-spatial perceptual areas. This student enrolled in the school for a two-hour session once a week to supplement her special education classes in the public school. Previous educational experiences

Three Selected Case Studies 169

during her life included those offerings in a special education setting.

Movement and Other Educational Experiences (First–Third Months)

Locomotor: Problem-solving situations and degrees of variations for each movement are those described in Chapter 8.

1. Walking.
2. Running.
3. Jumping.
4. Leaping.
5. Sliding.
6. Galloping.
7. Combinations of the above movements.

Basic Motor Skills.

1. Throwing.
2. Catching.
3. Hitting.

Various games situations were used for all of the above, since this student had a relatively high degree of skill.

Physiological Efficiency.

1. Muscular strength.
   a. Weight lifting (five-pound dumbbells) for ams and shoulders.
   b. Sit-ups for abdomen.
   c. Broad jump for the legs.
   d. Duck walk for the legs.
   e. Leg curls.
2. Muscular endurance.
   a. Squat jumps.
   b. Sit-ups.
   c. Push-ups.
   d. Crab walk.
   e. Bar hang.

3. Flexibility.
    a. Lower back and leg stretch (standing).
    b. Modified sit and reach.
4. Cardiovascular endurance.
    a. Run in place.
    b. All movements noted above under muscular strength and endurance were performed without a rest and in a relatively short period of time.
5. Relaxation.
    a. Head and neck.
    b. Arms.
    c. Trunk.
    d. Legs.
6. Posture.
    a. Abdominal wall.
    b. Legs.
    c. Feet.
7. Balance.
    a. Static—left and right foot balance.
    b. Dynamic—walking lines and Nelson Balance Test.
8. Speed of movement and reaction time.
    a. Red flag.
9. Agility.
    a. Quadrant jump.
    b. Obstacle course.
10. Power.
    a. Standing broad jump.

Perceptual-Motor Efficiency.

1. Laterality-midline.
    a. Verbal commands.
    b. Balance—static and dynamic.
2. Directionality.
    a. Exploration of external space.
    b. Beter-Cragin Oral Directions-Motor Response Checklist.

c. Reaction to a visual stimulus.
d. Kinesthetic awareness of direction.
e. Temporal relationships through creative and exploratory movements.
f. Beter-Cragin Perceptuo-Scope.

Selected Skills of Sports and Recreational Games.

1. Archery.
2. Badminton.
3. Basketball.
4. Bounce ball.
5. Darts.
6. Golf—putting.
7. Rhythms—creative movements to popular music.
8. Volleyball.

Other Selected Educational Experiences.

1. Arithmetic skills—addition and subtraction.
2. Reading comprehension—reading selected sections from various books.

Parent Conference and Progress Report. At the time of the conference this student had shown improvement in her perceptual-motor development and had increased her attention span considerably. She was also making steady progress in arithmetic and reading comprehension. Improvement was also shown in the areas of physiological efficiency.

Movement and Other Educational Experiences (Fourth–Sixth Months)

The program for this period was as follow:

1. Increased difficulty was introduced in all previously described movements under each section, utilizing more complex movements and conbinations of movements.

2. Sock It–Block It, tennis and dance (Tinikling) were new

sports activities engaged in, along with the continuation of skills previously mentioned.

3. Multiplication and problem-solving situations were presented in arithmetic.

4. Typing.

5. Working with money, using practical, problem-solving situations.

6. Continued work with reading comprehension.

Parent Conference and Progress Report. The student was able to recognize all of the coins, make change to a degree, and understand the basic concept of various amounts of money. Continued progress was being made in all other areas, particularly in the leisure-time skills.

Movement and Other Educational Experiences (Seventh–Ninth Months)

The activities for the last period are listed below.

1. All movement experiences as previously described were continued, but became more complex in nature.

2. Selected sports and recreational skills included the addition of tap dancing, kick ball, softball, dodge ball, card playing, bingo, creative dance movements and exploratory movements.

3. Selected educational experiences became more advanced and emphasis was placed on problem-solving experiences applicable to practical life situations.

Parent Conference and Progress Report. All areas of perceptual-motor development, physiological efficiency, and leisure time skills showed continued improvement. The student had reached the 4.6 grade level in vocabulary, 4.4 in comprehension and 3.2 in arithmetic. She had made considerable improvement in working with money and was able to make change without much hesitation.

Student 3

Student 3 was a six-year-old female Caucasian who had previously been diagnosed as having Laurence-Moon-Biedl syndrome. She was, at the time of enrollment, just starting a regular first-grade class in the public schools and was supplementing her education once a week in a two-hour session. Prior to beginning the supplementary program, this student displayed difficulties in all areas of perceptual-motor development.

Movement Experiences (First–Third Months)

Locomotor: The problem-solving situations and degrees of variation, as described in Chapter 8 were used for each movement.

1. Walking: Heel, toe, forward and backward on lines; walking on the balls of the feet fast and slowly.

2. Running: Forward, backward, slowly and quickly, controlling an object.

3. Jumping: Vertically and horizontally.

4. Hopping: Distance and height, forward and backward, changing feet and direction, slowly and quickly.

Basic Motor Skills.

1. Throwing: Underarm throw with large colored balls and bean bags at short distances.

2. Catching: Bouncing and catching a large ball; catching large balls thrown from short distances.

3. Kicking: Large balls from a stationary position.

Physiological Efficiency.

1. Muscular strength.
    a. Weight lifting with five-pound dumbbells.
    b. Sit-ups with assistance.
    c. Rope and duck walk.
2. Muscular endurance.
    a. Sit-ups with assistance.
    b. Trampoline.
    c. Crab walk.

3. Flexibility.
    a. Lower back and leg stretch from a sitting position.
    b. Trunk extension.
4. Cardiovascular endurance.
    a. Run in place.
    b. Movements described under muscular strength and endurance, performed without a rest and in a relatively short period of time.
    c. Trampoline.
5. Relaxation.
    a. Head and neck.
    b. Arms.
    c. Legs.
6. Balance.
    a. Static—left and right foot.

All movements described above utilized problem-solving situations and variations, as outlined in Chapter 7, as well as verbal commands.

Perceptual-Motor Efficiency.

1. Body-image.
    a. Identifying and locating body parts from verbal commands.
2. Laterality.
    a. Moving various body parts and segments from verbal commands.
    b. Static and dynamic balance.
3. Laterality-midline.
    a. Movements of body segments which require crossing the midline of the body.
    b. Balance.
4. Directionality.
    a. Exploration of external space.
    b. Beter-Cragin Bean Bag Test.
    c. Ball activities.
    d. Beter-Cragin Oral Directions-Motor Response Checklist.

        e. Activities utilizing visual, auditory, tactile and kinesthetic identification of direction.
    5. Temporal relationships.
        a. Creative movement experiences.
    6. Sensory efficiency.
        a. Beter-Cragin Perceptuo-Scope.

Parent Conference and Progress Report. This student was beginning to gain self-confidence and exhibited less tension in the performance of relatively simple tasks. She displayed an interest in movement experiences and as a result, made improvement in the physiological areas. Although progress was made in all areas at the end of three months, the student was still slightly behind the point at which she should have been for her chronological age.

Movement and Other Educational Experiences (Fourth–Sixth Months)

Locomotor.

1. All movements previously mentioned with increased degrees of difficulty and with combinations of locomotor movements were introduced.

2. Quarter turns and half turns were introduced in combination with other locomotor movements.

3. More emphasis was placed on exploratory and creative movements.

Basic Motor Skills: The same motor skills as previously mentioned were used with increased difficulty.

Physiological Efficiency.

1. Increased difficulty for all previously described movements.

2. Increased emphasis on static and dynamic balance.

Perceptual-Motor Efficiency.

1. Body-image.
    a. Movement experiences for understanding use of body parts.

2. Laterality and directionality.
   a. All movement experiences previously mentioned with increased difficulty.
3. Temporal relationships.
   a. Movement experiences as described in Chapter 8, under "Structured Activities."

Selected Skills of Sports and Recreational Games.
1. Horseshoes.
2. Ring toss.
3. Darts.
4. Putting.

Other Selected Educational Emperiences.
1. Puzzles.
2. Reading vocabulary and comprehension.

Parent Conference and Progress Report. At the end of the sixth month, this student's endurance for engaging in vigorous physical activities had increased substantially. Particularly was progesss made in the area of balance. She was able to make many necessary adjustments, had gained more confidence and maturity and generally, indicated more emotional stability than at the time of enrollment. She continued to show progress in the developmental areas, such as laterality, directionality and space relationships and was performing at a level close to her chronological age. Because of the fact that she was finding continued success in performing a variety of tasks, she was showing definite improvement in being able to cope with the first major challenge of her life—school.

Movement and Other Educational Experiences (Seventh–Ninth Months)

The final period was developed as follow:

1. All movements previously described under all sections, with varying degrees of increased difficulty and the addition of more complex movements.

2. Rope skipping without continuous movement.

3. Reading vocabulary and comprehension, number concepts and basic arithmetic skills, printing and tracing cursive letters.

Parent Conference and Progress Report. Improvement was shown in all areas. The major improvement was shown in the student's attitude toward facing new experiences. Where she would previously attempt to avoid new tasks, she now approached them with confidence and enthusiasm. She scored at the 2.1 grade level in reading and 2.2 level in arithmetic and was promoted to a regular second-grade class for the coming year in the public school she is attending.

SUMMARY

Perhaps more than in any other aspect, American educators have made their greatest accomplishments in the coining of provocative philosophical phrases. Failure to implement the philosophies, on the other hand, has caused their greatest disappointments. When the authors state that "Movement *is* what movement *does*," we are offering a deceptively simple educational philosophy. We would, therefore, hasten to caution the reader to examine the full implications of that statement.

Movement is a learning medium, but it will *do* only what it has been programed to do. We have suggested that movement experiences can provide the means for helping mentally retarded children learn to know themselves and the world in which they live. This is possible only if the person planning and guiding those experiences understands the nature and function of movement, and understands the child for whom the experiences are being planned.

Along with understanding the individual and the experiences offered to him, is the very essential element of understanding the outcome of engaging in those experiences. Because they have been classified as *mentally* retarded, people who deal with these children tend to ultimately focus their attention upon the mental aspects of their behavior. When innovative programs are studied, new techniques or methods tried, the results are invariably analyzed in light of progress made as indicated by the measurement of some aspect of intellectual functioning. Actually, these children are suffering from a developmental deficit which sends forth ripples into all channels of their total personality. The older they are chronologically, the more tangled the web of interlocking emotional and psychological factors affecting their behavior. It is true that the measurement of many important aspects of behavior is not yet possible in terms of statistical validity and reliability. To discount these aspects in analyzing outcomes because they cannot be quantitatively measured, however, is to do a grave disservice to the retarded and to our eventual understanding of the problems they face.

We have provided in this section three case studies to illustrate sample programs of movement experiences. These three students were selected because they provided extremes in terms of age and a variety in terms of etiology. Although they were not case studies in the research sense, we included a minimum of background information and a summary of progress made at the end of each three-month period. We would like to point out that the lack of statistical and quantitative data in the reports of progress is not entirely due to the fact that these were not intended to be scientific case studies. It is our contention that a report which states that substantial improvement was made in physiological efficiency is indicating a significant change in total behavior. To say that a six-year-old girl, fighting the vitally important struggle against shrinking from the unknown and threatening big world, has emerged self-confident and eager to explore is to reveal imformation which could conceivably influence the future course of her life. Would it have been of greater importance to state that her IQ had increased significantly? Academic achievement is certainly an important objective and is one of the outcomes we would hope would result from educational experiences. Unless we expect, plan for and recognize desirable changes in all areas of behavior, however, we are failing to *understand* the child we seek to help. Unless we expect, plan for and recognize the awkward becoming the synchronized, the hesitant becoming the bold, the watcher becoming the doer, the vacant stare becoming the gleeful shout, the shadowy world becoming the sunlit playground, then we are failing to *understand* movement.

BIBLIOGRAPHY

1. Alden, Florence D., and Top, Hilda: Experiment on the relation of posture of weight, vital capacity and intelligence. *Research Quarterly, 2*:38, 1931.
2. American Association for Health, Physical Education and Recreation: *Youth Fitness Test Manual.* Washington, D.C., AAHPER, 1965.
3. Ames, Louise Bates: Individuality of motor development. *Journal of the American Physical Therapy Association, 46*:121, 1966.
4. Association for Supervision and Curriculum Development (a department of the N.E.A.): Perceiving, behaving, becoming. *Yearbook.* Washington, D.C., 1962, p. 96.
5. Axline, Virginia M.: *Dibs In Search of Self.* New York, Ballantine, 1970, p. 20.
6. Ayres, A. Jean: Interrelation of perception, function and treatment. *Journal of the American Physical Therapy Association, 46*:741, 1966.
7. Bass, Ruth: An analysis of the components of tests of semi-circula canal function and of static and dynamic balance. *Research Quarterly, 10*:33, 1939.
8. Bell, Virginia Lee: *Sensorimotor Learning.* Pacific Palisades, Goodyear, 1970.
9. Bender, Jay, and Shea, Edward: *Physical Fitness: Tests and Exercises.* New York, Ronald, 1964.
10. Benoit, E. Paul: Extending the mind through the body. *Journal of Health, Physical Education and Recreation, 37*:28, 1966.
11. Berkeley, G.: Essay towards a new theory of vision. In Graser, A.C. (Ed.): *Selections From Berkeley.* Oxford, Clarendon Press, 1910.
12. Beter, Thais R.: The Effects of a Concentrated Physical Education Program and an Auditory and Visual Per-

ception Reading Program upon Academic Achievement, Intelligence, and Motor Fitness of Educable Mentally Retarded Children. Doctor's dissertation, Louisiana State University, 1969.
13. Bruner, Jerome S., Olver, Rose R., Greenfield, Patricia M., et al.: *Studies in Cognitive Growth.* New York, Wiley, 1966.
14. Clarke, H. Harrison: *Application of Measurement to Health and Physical Education,* 4th ed. Englewood Cliffs, Prentice-Hall, 1967.
15. ——— and Wickens, J. Stuart: Maturity, structural, strength, and motor ability growth curves of boys 9 to 15 years of age. *Research Quarterly, 33:*26, 1962.
16. Cohen, Leonard A.: Mechanisms of perception: Their development and function. *Perceptual-Motor Foundations: A Multidisciplinary Concern.* Washington, D.C., American Association for Health, Physical Education and Recreation, 1969.
17. Cooper, John M., and Glassow, Ruth B.: *Kinesiology.* St. Louis, Mosby, 1963, p. 114.
18. Cooper, Kenneth H.: *Aerobics.* New York, M. Evans & Co., 1968.
19. Cratty, Bryant J.: *Motor Activity and the Education of Retardates.* Philadelphia, Lea and Febiger, 1969.
20. Denhoff, Eric: Motor development as a function of perception. *Perceptual-Motor Foundations: A Multidisciplinary Concern.* Washington, D.C., American Association for Health, Physical Education and Recreation, 1969.
21. de Vries, Herbert A.: *Physiology of Exercise for Physical Education and Athletics.* Dubuque, W. C. Brown, 1966, pp. 37-41.
22. Drem, Liselot: *Who Can.* Frankfort, Germany, Wilhelm Limport, 1965.
23. Durant, Will: *The Story of Philosophy,* 2nd ed. New York, Simon and Schuster, 1961, p. 393.
24. Ebersole, Marylou, Kephart, Newell C., and Ebersole,

James B.: *Steps to Achievement for the Slow Learner.* Columbus, C.E. Merrill, 1968.
25. Enos, Francis A.: Emotional adjustment of mentally retarded children. *American Journal of Mental Deficiency, 65:*606, 1961.
26. Espenschade, Anna S., and Eckert, Helen M.: *Motor Development.* Columbus, C.E. Merrill, 1967.
27. ——— and others: Dynamic balance in adolescent boys. *Research Quarterly, 24:*270, 1953.
28. Gates, D. P., and Sheffield, R. P.: Tests of change of direction as measurement of different kinds of motor ability in boys of the 7th, 8th, and 9th grades. *Research Quarterly, 11:*136, 1940.
29. Glasscow, Ruth B.: Improvement of Motor Development and Physical Fitness in Elementary School Children. Cooperative Research Project No. 696, Microcard P.E. 708, p. 82. U.S. Office of Education, 1966.
30. Goldwaite, Joel E., and others: *Essentials of Body Health and Disease.* Philadelphia, Lippincott, 1952.
31. Hall, Elizabeth: A conversation with Jean Piaget and Barbel Inhelder. *Psychology Today, 3:*25, 1970.
32. Harvey, Patricia Ann: The Construction of a Rhythm Test Based on Motor Response for Women Physical Education Majors at North Texas State University. Unpublished master's thesis, North Texas State University, Denton, Texas, 1963.
33. Hoffman, Virginia: Relation of Selected Traits and Abilities to Motor Learning. Doctor's dessertation, Indiana University, 1955.
34. Hutchins, Gloria Lee: The relationship of selected strength and flexibility variables to the anterio-posterior posture of college women. *Research Quarterly, 36:*253, 1965.
35. Hutt, Max L., and Gibby, Robert Gwyn: *The Mentally Retarded Child.* Boston, Allyn and Bacon, 1965.
36. Ismail, A. H., and Gruber, J. J.: *Motor Aptitude and Intellectual Performance.* Columbus, C. E. Merrill, 1967.

37. Johnson, Barry L., and Nelson, Jack K.: *Practical Measurements for Evaluation in Physical Education.* Minneapolis Burgess, 1969.
38. Kennedy, Ruby J. R.: *The Social Adjustment of Morons in a Connecticut City.* Hartford, State Office Building, 1948.
39. Kephart, Newell C.: *The Slow Learner in the Classroom.* Columbus, C. E. Merrill, 1960.
40. Kirk, Samuel A.: *Educating Exceptional Children.* Boston, Houghton, 1962, pp. 110-111.
41. Lafuze, Marion: A study of the learning of fundamental skills by college freshman women of low motor ability. *Research Quarterly,* 22:156, 1951.
42. Lashley, Karl: In search of the engram. In Tibbets, Paul (Ed.): *Perception-Selected Readings in Science and Phenomenology.* Chicago, Quadrangle, 1969.
43. Lilly, Luella J.: *An Overview of Body Mechanics.* Westfield, Indiana, Peek, 1966.
44. Luria, Alexander R.: *The Role of Speech in the Regulation of Normal and Abnormal Behavior.* New York, Liveright, 1961.
45. ——— *The Mentally Retarded Child.* Oxford, Pergamon, 1963.
46. McDaniel, Clyde O. Jr.: Extra curricular activities as a factor in social acceptance among EMR students. *Mental Retardation,* 2:26, 1971.
47. Mayer, Jean: *Overweight, Causes, Cost and Control.* Englewood Cliffs, Prentice-Hall, 1968.
48. Mead, Barbara J.: Movement and rhythm. In Smith, Hope M. (Ed.): *Introduction to Human Movement.* Menlo Addison-Wesley, 1968.
49. Metheny, Eleanor: *Body Dynamics.* New York, McGraw-Hill, 1952.
50. ——— Only by moving their bodies. *Quest,* 2:47, 1964.
51. Miller, Augustus T.: Physiology of Exercise. St. Louis, Mosby, 1959.
52. Moriarity, Mary J., and Irwin, Leslie W.: A study of the

relationship of certain physical and emotional factors to habitual poor posture among school children. *Research Quarterly, 23*:221, 1952.
53. Nelson, Fred B.: *The Nelson Reaction Timer.* Instruction leaflet. P.O. Box 51987, Lafayette, La.
54. Oliver, James: The effect of physical conditioning exercises and activities on the mental characteristics of educationally subnormal boys. *British Journal of Educational Psychology, 28*:155, 1958.
55. Oberteuffer, Delbert: Some contributions of physical education to an educated life. In Patterson, Ann, and Hallberg, Edmond C.: *Background Readings for Physical Education.* New York, Holt, 1967, pp. 112-114.
56. Piaget, Jean: *Piaget—Sensori-Motor Intelligence and Cognitive Development.* New York, International, 1952.
57. President's Council on Physical Fitness. *Youth Physical Fitness.* Washington, D.C., U.S. Government Printing Office, 1967.
58. Robinson, Halbert B., and Robinson, Nancy M.: *The Mentally Retarded Child—A Psychological Approach.* New York, McGraw-Hill, 1965.
59. Sargent, L. W.: Some observations in the Sargent test of neuro-muscular efficiency. *American Physical Education Review, 29*:47, 1924.
60. Schilder, P.: *The Image and Appearance of the Human Body.* New York, International, 1935.
61. Scott, M. Gladys: Tests of kinesthesis. *Research Quarterly, 26*:324, 1955.
62. Sheldon, William H.: *Atlas of Men.* New York, Harper, 1954.
63. Shrader, Ray Anne: Action models for functional fitness. In Smith, Hope M. (Ed.): *Introduction to Human Movement.* Menlo Park, Addison-Wesley, 1968, pp. 112-114.
64. Shrader, Ray Anne: Learning to move skillfully. In Smith, Hope M. (Ed.): *Introduction to Human Movement.* Menlo Park, Addison-Wesley, 1968.

65. Skubic, Vera, and Hodgkins, Jean: Cardiovascular efficiency test for girls and women. *Research Quarterly*, *34*:191, 1963.
66. Slusher, Howard S., and Lockhart, Ailiene S.: *Anthology of Contemporary Readings*. Dubuque, W. C. Brown, pp. 28-40.
67. Smith, Hope M.: The nature of human movement. In Smith, Hope M. (Ed.): *Introduction to Human Movement*. Menlo Park, Addison-Wesley, 1968, p. 5.
68. Smith, Jean A.: Relation of certain physical traits and abilities to motor learning in elementary school children. *Research Quarterly*, *27*:228, 1956.
69. Smith J. R., and Hurst, J. G.: The relationship of motor activities and peer acceptance of mentally retarded children. *American Journal of Mental Deficiency*, *66*:81, 1961.
70. Spindler, Evelyn B.: Prevalence of and correlations between physical defects and their coincidence with functional disorders. *Research Quarterly*, *2*:36, 1931.
71. Stein, Julian U.: Motor function and physical fitness of the mentally retarded: A critical review. *Rehabilitation Literature*, *24*:230, 1963.
72. Steinhaus, Arthur: *Toward an Understanding of Health and Physical Education*. Dubuque, W. C. Brown, 1963.
73. ——— Your muscles see more than your eyes. *Journal of Health, Physical Education and Recreation*, *37*:38, 1966.
74. The American Association on Mental Deficiency: *A Manual on Terminology and Classification in Mental Retardation*. Monograph supplement to *American Journal of Mental Deficiency*, 2nd ed., 1961.
75. Trippet, Frank: The ordeal of fun. *Look Magazine*, *33*:25, 1969.
76. Ulrich, Celeste: *The Social Matrix of Physical Education*. Prentice-Hall, Englewood Cliffs, 1968, p. 115.
77. Wells, Katherine F., and Dillon, Evelyn K.: The sit and reach—a test of back and leg flexibility. *Research Quarterly*, *23*:118, 1952.

78. Whelan, Thomas P.: A Factor Analysis of Tests of Balance and Semicircular-Canal Function. Doctor's dissertation, State University of Iowa, 1955.
79. Whitehurst, Katusob E.: What movement means to the young child. *Journal of Health, Physical Education and Recreation, 42:*34, 1971. Taken from Conference Report by Curtis, D. M.: The Young Child: The Significance of Motor Development.
80. Wiebe, Vernon R.: A study of tests of kinesthesis. *Research Quarterly, 25:*222, 1954.
81. Willgoose, Carl E.: *Evaluation in Health Education and Physical Education.* New York, McGraw-Hill, 1961.

APPENDIX

SELF-OPINION TEST
QUESTIONS AND KEY

1. Are you good at making things with your hands?   Y
2. Can you draw well?   Y
3. Are you strong?   Y
4. Do you like the way you look?   Y
5. Do your friends make fun of you?   N
6. Are you handsome/pretty?   Y
7. Do you have trouble making friends?   N
8. Do you like school?   Y
9. Do you wish you were different?   N
10. Are you sad most of the time?   N
11. Are you the last to be chosen in games?   N
12. Do girls like you?   Y
13. Are you a good leader in games and sports?   Y
14. Are you clumsy?   N
15. In games do you watch instead of play?   N
16. Do boys like you?   Y
17. Are you happy most of the time?   Y
18. Do you have nice hair?   Y
19. Do you play with younger children a lot?   N
20. Is reading easy for you?   Y

Courtesy of Cratty, Bryant J.: *Motor Activity and the Education of Retardates.* Philadelphia, Lea and Febiger, 1969.

GLOSSARY

Accent—Special emphasis; increased force of rhythmic events.
Anthropometric—Science of measuring the human body and its parts.
Articulations—Connections between two bones, joints.
Balance—Ability of an individual to hold a stationary position (static), or his ability to maintain balance during movement (dynamic).
Beat—Steady, continuing basic count of rhythmic events.
Cardiovascular Endurance—The ability to sustain a series of repetitions of any activity without unduly taxing the systems which furnish the fuel and oxygen to the muscles.
Conceptualization—Relations of what is perceived.
Constitutional Psychology—The study of the psychological aspects of human behavior as they are related to the morphological and physiological aspects of the body.
Disequilibrium—A state of imbalance or unequality between opposing forces.
Exceptional Child—That child who deviates from the average or normal child in mental, physical, or social characteristics to such an extent that he requires a modification of school practices or special educational services in order to develop to his maximum capacity.
Experiences—Everything and anything that an individual has encountered or that has happened to him.
Exploratory Movements—Attempts to answer questions (problem solving) through free, expressive movements in time and space.
Extension—Movement of a body segment by which the adjacent parts are brought into straighter alignment.
Flexibility—A wide range of movement or ability to bend in various directions.
Flexion—Movement in a joint by which the two adjacent segments approach each other.
Force—The effort which one body exerts on another. In the human organism, the primary source of force is the individual's strength.

Glossary

Golgi Tendon Organ—Found in the musculotendinous junction and throughout the perimysial connective tissue.

Inhibitory Processes—Those processes involved with modifying the reception, conduction and integration of all sensory signals to the degree that some will be perceived and others rejected by the nervous system.

Locomotor Movements—Activities which move the body through space in definite patterns (running, skipping, and so forth).

Morphology—The branch of biology dealing with the form and structure of animals and plants.

Motor Learning—Permanent change in motor performance brought about through practice.

Motor Performance—Immediate and short-term motor behavior.

Muscle Spindle—Widely distributed throughout muscle tissue, it consists of a connective sheath of intrafusal muscle fibers and sensory-end organs.

Muscular Endurance—The ability of specific muscle groups to exert external force in successive repetitions.

Overt Behavior—Observable expressions of an individual through acts, interactions and reactions in any situation.

Pacinian Corpuscle—Found concentrated in the region of the joints and sheaths of tendons and muscles; are pressed upon when muscles contract.

Perceiving—Awareness of objects or data through the sense medium.

Perceptual-Motor—Motor behavior which is dependent upon sensory cues and the perceptual process.

Proprioceptors—Receptors which are related to kinesthetic sensations. They include the muscle spindle, the Golgi tendon organ and the Ruffini endings found in joint capsules.

Psychosomatic—Relationship of mind and body.

Pubescent—State of sexual maturation.

Reaction Time—Interval of time between the stimulus and the individual's response.

Rebound Skipping—An extra bounce is taken each time the feet contact the surface, similar to a one-two count.

Response—That which is said or done.

Reticular Formation—Responsible in part for arousal of the cortex. It can receive and reject sensory information.

Sensory Modality—The particular apparatus connected with the reception and transmission of sense impressions.

Side-Stride Position—An individual stands in a stationary position with the feet approximately twelve inches apart and parallel to each other. The feet are side by side, about shoulder-width apart.

Skill—Combinations of specific, sequented movements in performance of any act.

Stimulus—Any action or agent which causes or changes activities of an organ or organs.

Straight Skipping—The feet do not rebound from the surface; the individual skips on the balls of the feet without an extra bounce on a count of one.

Strength—An individual's ability to exert external force.

Syndrome—A number of symptoms together which affect behavior.

Tension—At any given time during contraction, the length of the muscle determines how much internal force or tension it can generate. *Example:* During isotonic contraction, there is one level of tension throughout the contraction.

Vestibular—A system involved with kinesthesis, balance and postural reflexes. It is a system related to the sense of motion, the position of the head in space and to the inner ear.

INDEX

A

AAHPER, 49, 50, 77
AAMD, 13–14
Age, 30–32
Agility, 60, 123
Alden, Florence D., 29
Ames, Louise B., 13, 23
Angling, 158
Anthropometric measurement, 33–35
Archery, 153
Association for Supervision and Curriculum Development, 166
Auditory Efficiency Test, 98
Axline, Virginia M., 7
Ayres, A. Jean, 20

B

Badminton, 154
Balance, 60, 117, 118, 119
Basketball, 155
Bass, Ruth, 115
Behavior
 individual, 12
 movement, 18
 social patterns, 149
Bell, Virginia Lee, 80–81
Benoit, E. Paul, 6
Berkeley, G., 16
Beter, Thais R., 116
Beter-Cragin
 Bean Bag Test, 89
 Modified Bean Bag Test, 91
 Modified Test of Horizontal and Linear Space, 70
 Perceptuo-Scope, 146
 Sock It Block It, 158
 Test of Oral Directions-Motor Responses, 88
Body image, 82–83, 138
Body type, 35
Bowling, 154
Bruner, Jerome S., 82–83
Burpee Test, 61

C

Cardiovascular efficiency, 41, 108
Chin-ups, 48
Circuit training, 126
Clarke, H. H., 31–32
Cohen, Leonard A., 80
Cooper, John M., 24
Cooper Walk/Run Program, 109
Cratty, Bryant J., 116, 151

D

Dart throwing, 157
Deck tennis, 157
Denhoff, Eric, 19
deVries, Herbert, 68
Directionality, 87, 140
Distance perception jump, 73
Dodge run, 123
Drem, Liselot, 102–103
Durant, Will, 3

E

Ectomorphy, 36
Endomorphy, 35
Enos, Francis A., 150
Espenschade, Anna, 22, 116

F

Flexed-Arm Hang, 49
Flexibility, 44, 107
Folk dance, 158
Football, 156

G

Gates, D. P., 123
Gator ball, 156
Gibby, Robert G., 13
Glasscow, R. B., 129
Glassow, Ruth, 24
Goldwaite, Joel E., 24
Golf, 155
Gravity Test, 25
Grip Strength Test, 53
Growth, 22
Gruber, J. J., 129

H

Harvard Step Test, 42
Harvey Rhythm Test, 93
Height, 32–33
Hockey, 156
Hodgkins, Jean, 42
Hoffman, Virginia, 115
Horizontal Linear Space Test, 68
Horseshoe pitching, 157
Hurst, J. G., 150
Hutchins, Gloria L., 29
Hutt, Max L., 13

I

Interval training, 127
Irwin, Leslie W., 30
Ismail, A. H., 129

J

Johnson, Barry L., 42, 45, 48, 50, 55, 62, 65, 75, 107, 119

K

Kennedy, Ruby, 150
Kephart, Newell C., 19, 83, 92, 115, 128, 146
Kinesthetic perception, 5, 67
Kirk, Samuel A., 150

L

Lafuze, Marion, 116
Lashley, Karl, 88
Laterality, 85–87, 139
Leisure-time activities, 153
Lilly, Luella J., 112
Locomotor patterns, 130
Luria, Alexander R., 129

M

McDaniel, Clyde O., 150
Maturation, 22
Mayer, Jean, 34
Mead, Barbara J., 92–93, 142
Medicine ball put, 75
Mental retardation, 13–14
Mesomorphy, 36
Metheny, Eleanor, 4, 7, 23
Miller, Augustus, 24
Modified Sit and Reach Test, 45
Moriarity, Mary J., 30
Motor
  performance, 20, 60
  planning, 19
  skills, 134
Movement
  basic patterns, 20
  behavior, 18
  objectives, 7–10
  philosophy, 3–7
Muscle Shortening, 27–29
Muscular Endurance, 48, 106

N

Nelson, Jack K., 42, 45, 48, 50, 55, 62, 75, 107, 119
Nelson Balance Test, 65
Nelson Hand Reaction Test, 76
Nelson Speed of Movement Test, 78

O

Oberteuffer, Delbert, 6
Obesity, 34
Obstacle run, 124
Oliver, James, 150

Index

P

Perception theories, 15–18
Perceptual-motor development, 19, 80, 128
Physiological functioning, 20, 41, 102
Piaget, Jean, 6, 16, 81, 130
Pinch Test, 34
Ping-Pong, 157
Ponderal Index, 37
Posture, 23, 112
Power, 74, 125
President's Council on Fitness, 115
Pubescent development, 32

Q

Quadrant jump, 63

R

Reaction time, 76, 120
Relaxation, 110
Rhythm, 92, 142
Robinson, Halbert B., 129
Robinson, Nancy M., 129
Ruler Test, 35

S

Sargent, L. W., 125
Schilder, P., 83
Scott, M. Gladys, 73
Sensory efficiency, 98, 146
Shea, Edward, 114
Sheffield, R. P., 123
Sheldon, William H., 35, 37
Shrader, Ray A., 25–28, 110–111
Shuffleboard, 157
Side Step Test, 62
Sit-ups, 50
Skubic, Vera, 42
Smith, Hope M., 41
Smith, Jean A., 116
Smith, J. R., 150
Softball, 156
Speed of movement, 76, 121
Spindler, Evelyn B., 30
Spring Scale Tests, 55
Square dance, 158
Squat jumps, 51
Standing broad jump, 74
Stein, Julian, 128
Steinhaus, Arthur, 5, 68
Strength, muscular, 52, 103
Swimming, 155

T

Tactile Efficiency Test, 100
Temporal relationships, 92, 142
Tennis, 155
Top, Hilda, 29
Trippet, Frank, 6

U

Ulrich, Celeste, 149

V

Vertical jump, 125
Vertical Linear Space Test, 70
Visual Efficiency Test, 99
Volleyball, 157

W

Weight, 32
Wells Sit and Reach Test, 47
Whelan, Thomas P., 115
Whitehurst, Katusob, 161
Wickens, J. S., 31
Wiebe, Vernon, 68–70
Willgoose, Carl, 38–39